An Economic History of Liberal Italy

The recent growth in Italy's economy has been spectacular and has received wide attention. However, the origins of this success have been less well understood, particularly in the Anglophone world. This book examines Italy's economic history from its Unification in 1850 to the end of the First World War. Particular attention is paid to the extent to which Italy exhibits the features of Kuznets's model of 'modern economic growth'.

An Economic History of Liberal Italy begins with a quantitative assessment of Italy's long-term growth in this period. All of the main relevant variables – including production, consumption, investment, foreign trade, government spending, and welfare – are discussed. The book proceeds through a chronological account of the developments of the economy during this period, and concludes with a critical survey of the relevant historiography.

Throughout the book emphasis is given to structural changes, to developments in the main industries, to the relations between different sectors of the economy, and to economic policies.

Giovanni Toniolo is Professor of Economics at the University of Venice, and is one of the leading authorities on Italy's economic growth. He is Visiting Fellow of St. Anthony's College, Oxford, and Editor of *Rivista di Storia Economica*. He has written many articles on economic history, and is the author of *L'Economia dell'Italia fascista* (The Italian economy during Fascism), 1980.

An Economic History of Liberal Italy
1850–1918

Gianni Toniolo

translated by
Maria Rees

ROUTLEDGE
London and New York

First published 1990 by Routledge
11 New Fetter Lane, London EC4P 4EE

Simultaneously published in the USA and Canada
by Routledge
a division of Routledge, Chapman and Hall, Inc.
29 West 35th Street, New York NY 10001

© 1990 Gianni Toniolo

Typeset by Pat and Anne Murphy, Highcliffe-on-Sea, Dorset
Printed and bound in Great Britain by
Mackays of Chatham PLC, Chatham, Kent

British Library Cataloguing in Publication Data

Toniolo, Gianni, *1942–*
    An economic history of liberal Italy 1850–1918.
    1. Italy. Economic development, 1968–1986
    I. Title   II. [Storia economica dell'Italia liberale
    1850–1918. *English*]
    330.945'0927

    ISBN 0-415-03500-7

Library of Congress Cataloging-in-Publication Data

Toniolo, Gianni, 1942–
    [Storia economica dell'Italia liberale, 1850–1918. English]
    An economic history of liberal Italy, 1850–1918 / by Gianni
Toniolo; translation by Maria Rees.
        p. cm.
    Translation of: Storia economica dell'Italia liberale, 1850–1918.
    Includes bibliographical references.
    ISBN 0-415-03500-7
    1. Italy—Economic conditions—1849–1870.   2. Italy—Economic
conditions—1870–1918. 3. Italy—Economic policy.   I. Title.
HC305.T54713   1990   89-35967
330.945'083—dc20   CIP

To Paolo,
'between the lesser mountains
and the greater'

Contents

Contents

Foreword

'The economist is concerned with the future as well as with the past but it is from the past that he has to begin'

John Hicks

According to American Express Bank, by the end of this century, Italy's GNP will be the highest in Western Europe (*Euromoney*, June 1989). As an economic historian I am not inclined to prophecy; however, it is noteworthy that in the late 1980s international statistics from various sources show that income *per capita* in Britain and in Italy are about of the same order of magnitude (and there is no denying that the British economy has done particularly well in the second part of the decade). In historical perspective, this appears to be an extraordinary achievement for Italy. On the eve of the First World War, such a performance could not have been anticipated by Giolitti, even in his wildest dreams, or taken by Lloyd George as anything but a joke.

In the English speaking world, the Italian case of 'modern economic growth' has not received the attention it deserves as an exceptional success story. The author hopes that the present book will contribute to a better understanding of that story. True: Italy's best economic performances were recorded after the end of the Second World War, when most of the 'catching-up' with the advanced countries of Western Europe took place. It is however difficult to understand fully the rapid development of the last forty years, its uneven nature, its pronounced dualism, its many contradictions, without taking seriously John Hick's advice that it is from the past that we have to begin.

It was between the revolutions of 1848–9 and the Peace of Versailles that 'modern economic growth' – as defined and described by Simon Kuznets – slowly took place and began to transform the economy of the Italian Peninsula in a way that proved to be irreversible. This long spell of time is often referred to by historians as that of 'Liberal Italy': it begins with the granting of modern Constitutions and ends with the turmoil that brought Fascism to power.

This book provides an introduction to the macroeconomic history of Liberal Italy. Its framework derives from the lectures I gave on the subject at Ca'Foscari (the University of Venice) during the last decade as part of my course on the economic history of Europe since the First Industrial Revolution. It takes, therefore, substantially the form of a textbook aimed at introducing future economists and businessmen to the origins of 'modern economic growth' in Italy. I was, however, happily surprised to see that the Italian edition was also well received by history students and by the general public.

The book is divided into three parts. The first (Chapters 1 to 4*) reviews the quantitative evidence of trends and cycles in the main macro-variables pertaining to output, demand, banking and finance, welfare, and productivity. The second (Chapters 5 to 11) provides a brief account of the economic events that are crucial for the understanding of Italy's 'modern economic growth'. The last part (Chapter 12) is devoted to historiography: it deals with the main interpretations of the economic events of Liberal Italy provided thus far by historians.

As a student of Gerschenkron, I was deeply influenced by his thought. Ten years ago I would have written a book much more influenced by his theses (or hypotheses) than this one. In particular, economic backwardness would have played a more important role as *the* explanatory variable for most of the individual behaviours and social choices that characterize the period. Indeed, Italy was a backward country since the economic crisis of the seventeenth century and I still feel that such backwardness is considerably relevant as an *explanatory* variable of the characteristics of Italy's economic development. But the study of Italian economic history has made considerable progress during the last two decades and many of its findings are not consistent with a Gerschenkronian approach. Accounting for these has resulted in my pouring a good deal of water into the strong wine of the great Russian Master.

This book is based on the best historical statistics available in the late 1980s: the author is confident that it provides a rather accurate picture of the 'state of the art' at this date. At the same time he must warn the reader that the progress made so far by quantitative economic history of Italy is important but not yet satisfactory.

* Financial support from CNR for research incorporated in Chapters 1 to 4 is gratefully acknowledged.

National accounting statistics – upon which part of this book had necessarily to be based – were produced in 1957: they do not meet the current standards of the field and are in need of revision. The quantification of productivity, welfare, standards of living, employment, and unemployment is an infant industry. The so-called 'questione meridionale' (southern question) has filled several bookshelves while generating surprisingly few acceptable statistics. Progress, however, is continuing: a small but highly qualified group of economic historians is currently working on improving the quality and coverage of Italian historical statistics. Their names appear so often in the pages of this book that they do not need to be repeated here: each of them knows how large an intellectual debt I owe him. My confidence in the progress of their work is such that, at the risk of upsetting my excellent publisher, I am prepared to bet that this book will soon be obsolete.

Ca'Foscari, Università di Venezia

Tables

Chapter one

Growth of product

Modern economic growth

Between the revolutions of 1848−9 and the Peace of Versailles the Italian economy underwent most of the transformations that typically characterize the first phases of 'modern economic growth'.[1] Until a few years ago, scholars tried to pinpoint and describe an 'industrial revolution',[2] a 'take-off',[3] a 'big spurt',[4] but these terms are now disappearing from the economic historian's vocabulary: they are imaginative but analytically ambiguous.

Kuznets uses the term 'modern economic growth' to describe 'the current epoch of spreading application of science to processes of production and social organization'[5] and empirically identifies such growth 'with sustained high rates of increase in per capita product'.[6]

Kuznets' units of observation are 'those large human societies with sufficient political independence and often overriding sovereignty to make their own decisions on basic economic and related issues':[7] in practice, the modern nation−state. The Italian peninsula − for Metternich a mere 'geographical expression' − gained its full independence from foreign powers and was unified into a single state after the wars of 1859−60. The Kingdom of Italy was proclaimed on 21 March 1861. The Constitution, given by King Carlo Alberto of Savoy to his Piedmontese subjects in 1848, applied to the Kingdom throughout the period covered by this book, granting Italian citizens personal freedom and giving them those political institutions that characterized the liberal democracies of the nineteenth century. These institutions did not survive the social unrest that broke out after the First World War and ended with the Fascist March on Rome (October 1922). Liberal Italy is, therefore, an appropriate entity to be studied in the framework of modern economic growth. One must not forget, however, that there might be excellent reasons − such as those suggested by

1

Pollard[8] – for analysing more homogeneous economic regions; in the case of Italy these reasons seem to be particularly valid in the light of the pronounced economic gap between the north and the south, which is one of the characteristics peculiar to the Italian economy.

According to Kuznets, modern economic growth is characterized by several distinctive features. First, high rates of increase in per capita income, ranging from less than 15 to about 30 per cent per decade, and an increase in population of about 10 per cent per decade, both rates being much higher than in pre-modern times. Second, the high rate of rise in per capita income is due primarily to improvements in quality, not quantity, of inputs. Third, increased efficiency characterizes all productive sectors, affecting all components of society and the underlying institutional arrangements. Fourth, the sectorial origin of aggregate output shows a decline in the share of agriculture, rises in the shares of manufacturing and public utilities, and shifts, within manufacturing, from less to more durable products. Such trends in the sectorial distribution of aggregate output reflect changes both in final demand and in technology. The latter does not affect all sectors in the same way. Fifth, a similar pattern of change takes place in the sectorial allocation of the labour force. Sixth, gross capital formation rises from about 10 to about 20 per cent of gross domestic product. Lastly, the welfare of all social groups or classes increases but relative inequalities have only been moderately reduced, if at all.[9]

The changes in production and consumption patterns characterizing modern economic growth are reflected in the social and political organization of societies and result in profound changes in the prevailing value system. Such changes are sometimes referred to as the 'modernization process', thus giving an implicitly positive meaning to the word 'modern'. However, it is extremely difficult to speak of 'modernization' in an unequivocal fashion, given the multiplicity and complexity of non-economic variables implicit in this concept and the fact that some of these variables – unlike economic growth – have proven far from irreversible. Nineteenth century liberals thought that economic development and democracy went hand-in-hand and that they were actually two sides of the same coin; the twentieth century has amply disproven this belief. As for value judgements, it is perhaps possible to find wide consensus in considering as positive an increase in the amount of material goods at the average individual's disposal, a shorter and easier working life, and a lengthening of life expectancy. The same consensus is not found in judging as positive the social, cultural, and anthropological changes which accompanied the transformation of traditional societies and the spread of modern economic growth. This is why, throughout this book, we shall use Kuznets' simple and perhaps unimaginative definition rather than the broader but ill-defined term of 'modernization'.

Kuznets sees the great migrations, the occupational shifts, the process of urbanization, the redistribution of economic power among productive sectors and social groups, which accompany modern economic growth as potentially destabilizing for society as a whole. A national consensus that would limit frictions and preserve the political strength of the state assumes, therefore, great importance in explaining the success of a given country in the achievement of modern economic growth. In discussing the economic history of Italy one has to bear in mind that national unity and liberal democracy were new and fragile when modern economic growth took its first steps in the Italian peninsula. The quantitative and qualitative limits of such growth must therefore be examined in the light of the country's social and political history.

Growth of gross domestic product

Estimates of Italy's National Accounts for the period 1861–1918 are far from satisfactory. They were produced in 1957 by the *Istituto Centrale di Statistica* (ISTAT),[10] and marginally revised, corrected, and integrated during the second half of the 1960s by a working group headed by Giorgio Fuà.[11] The reconstruction of the time series of the main aggregates of national accounting for periods in which these were not available is always an exercise subject to wide margins of indetermination, however well it may be conducted both from an economic and from a historical point of view. Without going into technical details which would lead us away from the purpose of this volume,[12] one need only consider the problems of theory connected with the very concept of individual and collective welfare, the problems of the measurement of capital stocks and flows, as well as the practical difficulty in dealing with the complex index-number problems that arise when comparing sets of goods whose relative prices over time inevitably change, and in estimating the value of new products (a particularly frequent case in the period under consideration).[13] For reasons such as these the use of time series of national accounting always requires methodological awareness and a knowledge of the techniques employed in the reconstruction of the aggregates being studied.

This latter condition cannot always be satisfied by those studying the Italian case for the good reason that the original work of ISTAT gives very few explanations of the methods used and often

Table 1.1 Italy's Gross Domestic Product 1861–1925 (average annual growth rates at constant prices)

Period	GDP	GDP per capita
1861–76	0.9	0.0
1876–88	0.5	−0.2
1888–96	0.8	0.1
1896–1908	2.7	2.1
1908–13	2.8	2.0
1913–22	0.4	0.0
1922–5	5.1	4.1

Sources: GDP: P. Ercolani, 'Documentazione statistica di base', in G. Fuà (ed.), *Lo sviluppo economico in Italia*, Milano: Angeli, 1969, vol. III, pp. 401–2. Population: ISTAT, *Sommario di statistiche storiche*, Rome: Poligrafico dello Stato, 1958, p. 38.

very little information on the primary sources for the elementary data on which the aggregates were based. In these circumstances, the group led by Fuà was faced with the alternatives of either accepting the basic series already in existence and making minor technical adjustments trying to update it technically or beginning the basic research work all over again. With the resources then available, the group opted for the first alternative: there were interesting improvements to some of the individual series – such as those relating to the stock of capital – without altering the essence of the overall picture offered by the preceding work of ISTAT. More than twenty years have passed since then without any need being felt, in Italy, to produce time series of national accounting qualitatively comparable to those existing in a growing number of countries. Some important research is being done, but its results – which we shall take into account – do not as yet allow an overall revision of the aggregate estimates. Given the 'state of the art' there are only two possible options: either to refuse any quantification and take refuge in qualitative intuition or to accept, once again, the use of the ISTAT series as reviewed by Fuà and his group.[14] We have opted for the second alternative.

If we go by the ISTAT–Fuà estimates, Italy's real GDP rose between 1861 and 1925 at an average annual compound rate of 1.4 per cent. The figure for the period 1861–1913 is only slightly higher (1.5 per cent). Taking into account an annual growth of 0.7 per cent in population, there would be an increase in per capita income of around 0.8 per cent per decade. This value is considerably below the threshold established by Kuznets for the determination of modern economic growth. Examining the series for gross domestic product more closely one notices that its trend accelerates considerably around the mid-1890s. During the first thirty-five years after the

Unification, per capita GDP fluctuated around an essentially stationary trend: the quantity of goods and services produced barely kept up with the demographic increase.[15] Between 1896 and 1925, on the contrary, per capita income rose, on average, by 1.6 per cent each year.

The existing series would indicate, therefore, that modern economic growth, as Kuznets sees it, began in Italy around the middle of the final decade of the last century; more than thirty years after the political unification of the country.

Agricultural production

The first two population censuses, in 1861 and 1871, are unreliable and comparable neither with each other nor with those which followed: a breakdown of the labour force by sectors may, therefore, be attempted only from 1881 onwards.[16] At that date, agriculture retained 59 per cent of the total labour force. By 1911 this share had fallen by only four percentage points. It was only in the 1930s that the agricultural work force fell below 50 per cent of the total, and only in the years after the Second World War, would there be that rapid fall in the number of those working in agriculture, which characterizes each process of economic growth. For the whole period 1861–1918 Italy's agricultural sector continued to be of greater relative importance than England's had been during the second half of the eighteenth century.

Agricultural output increased very slowly in the first thirty-five years after the Unification: taking the five-year averages for 1861–5 and 1896–1900, the annual growth rate was only 0.4 per cent. If the ISTAT data are accurate, domestic production of foodstuffs was not able to keep up with demographic increase which, in the same period, was around 0.7 per cent.

Italian agriculture seemed to revive from the last years of the nineteenth century onwards: the growth rate of 2.1 per cent between 1896–1900 and 1911–13 is remarkable both when compared with other countries and with other periods of rapid growth in Italy. For example, during the so-called 'economic miracle' (1950–64) the Italian gross agricultural product grew at an average annual rate (2.3 per cent) much the same as that during the Giolitti era. Between 1911–13 and 1923–5, however, the growth of agricultural production felt the effects of the First World War: the rate of growth being around 0.7 per cent per annum.

Given this sector's importance for the entire Italian economic system of the time, it should come as no surprise that its performance paralleled, more or less, that of national income. This point is important when it comes to discussing the factors which either promoted or delayed growth in industry.

Industrial production

Modern economic growth is by its very nature associated with the process of industrialization. It is not by chance that the transition from a traditional to a modern economy has been called 'industrial revolution'. The process of industrialization characterizing modern economic growth differs greatly from country to country. The transition from cottage industry to factory system often takes place over a long period of time and has its own features specific to sector and geographical area, and is sometimes called 'proto-industrialization'.

In 1861 there were in Italy a number of 'modern' factories which each employed several hundreds of workers throughout the year. Many industrial products, however, still came from cottage industries, artisans' workshops, or from production units which, though organized along factory system lines, displayed substantial seasonal fluctuations in employment. In many cases it is not easy to draw a clear distinction between agricultural activity and manufacturing production and the actual gathering of statistical data suffers from this blurring. A case in point is provided by the early population censuses: since many workers were involved throughout the year in both agricultural and industrial activities, the answers to questions relating to their occupation varied according to the season in which the census was taken.

Thus, the estimates for industrial production for the first decades after the Unification rely, even more so than those for more recent periods, on what can be inferred from the few and imprecise sectorial investigations and from a series of indirect indicators. A few indices of industrial production existed before the publication of the ISTAT series. Reference can be made to the better-known of such indices – that of Gerschenkron.[17] Another important index of industrial output was produced by Fenoaltea.[18] He is now working on estimates of Italy's industrial production for the years 1861–1913: it is likely that when his work is finished many of the conclusions of this book will have to be revised.

According to the ISTAT estimates, when the Kingdom of Italy was proclaimed, manufacturing industry was equal to 16 per cent of GDP. The construction and mining sectors each amounted to little more than 1 per cent of GDP. In 1925 manufacturing production represented around a quarter of gross domestic product. During those sixty-five years the average annual rate of growth in

Table 1.2 Industrial production in Italy 1862–1925 (average annual compound rates at constant prices)

Period	ISTAT indices (manufacturing industry)	Fenoaltea indices
1861–1925	2.2	—
1861–1913	2.0	3.5
1861–96	1.0	2.2
1896–1913	4.0	6.2
1896–1925	4.2	—
1861–76	1.7	1.6
1876–88	0.8	5.4
1888–96	0.0	– 1.3
1896–1908	5.2	7.9
1908–13	1.4	2.3
1913–20	0.0	—
1920–5	7.1	—

Sources: ISTAT, *Indagine statistica sullo sviluppo del reddito nazionale in Italia dal 1861 al 1956*, Annali di Statistia, Rome, 1957; S. Fenoaltea, 'Italy', in P.K. O'Brien (ed.), *Railways and the Economic Development of Western Europe*, London: Macmillan, 1983.

the manufacturing sector was to be around 2.2 per cent, that is around one-and-a-half times the growth rate of national income.

In industry too, the year 1896 coincided with an important trend acceleration in production, which is clearly visible in both the ISTAT and Fenoaltea indices. From many other points of view, the two series diverge radically as one can see in Table 1.2. Particular attention should be paid to the considerable difference in long-term growth rates (1861–1913): ISTAT's being little more than half of Fenoaltea's. This gap is explained mainly by a totally different assessment of the 1880s and from Fenoaltea's far more optimistic estimate of development during the Giolitti era. Observing the individual sub-periods in Table 1.2, it can be seen that the two indices agree on the growth rate of Italian industry during the years that the Right was in power (1861–76); tell an entirely different industrial history of the 1880s; agree in essence both on the existence of a serious depression between 1887–8 and the fall of Crispi, and in singling out, around this date, a turning point after which an important industrial development phase took place for which, however, the two indices offer different estimates. It should be added, on the basis of the ISTAT data only, that this long favourable cycle seems to have continued at least until 1925, with

Table 1.3 Growth in manufacturing production 1896–1925 (average annual growth rates at constant prices)

Period	Food	Textiles	Metal	Egineering	Chemicals
1896–1925	3.3	2.1	7.4	6.9	10.5
1896–1908	5.9	4.4	9.9	11.7	16.1
1908–13	2.6	−0.4	8.3	2.6	5.0
1913–25	1.1	0.8	4.5	4.2	6.6

Source: P. Ercolani, 'Documentazione statistica di base', in G. Fuà (ed.) *Lo sviluppo economico in Italia*, Milan: Franco Angeli, 1969, vol. III.

an interruption during the last two years of the First World War and the immediate post-war period.

Given the caution with which Fenoaltea considers his own 1967 index, it is difficult to favour either quantitative assessment of Italy's industrial history. The problem of the 1880s is crucial for some of the existing interpretations of the process of Italian industrialization (see Chapter twelve). As for the quantification of the Giolittian 'boom', it seems obvious, for the purposes of a comparative evaluation of Italy's performance, that a growth rate of 8 per cent is quite a different matter than one of 5 per cent; in the first case we would be faced by an almost exceptional development in the context of nineteenth-century Europe, in the second there would be only a good performance well within the average of other similar cases.

Some ideas of the trend in the main manufacturing sectors can be gathered only from the rather approximate estimates of the Fuà group[19] for the years after 1896: these are summarized in Table 1.3. The resulting picture is consistent with the expectations of those studying modern economic growth: capital intensive industries with a high rate of technical progress developed far more rapidly than 'traditional' ones. Particular attention should be paid to the rapid growth in the engineering and chemical industries which were to be, at least until the end of the 1960s, two of the most dynamic sectors in the Italian economic system.

Services

All the current talk of a service economy rapidly replacing the industrial economy which generated and supported modern economic growth in the Western world during the last two hundred years, should not mislead: in a historical perspective, the overall performance of the service sector was not exceptional. The case of Liberal Italy seems clear on this point. The contribution of services, excluding the civil service, to GNP has remained unvaried at around 30 per cent.

The Fuà group presented a disaggregate estimate for five large service categories. Transport and communications and Credit and insurance, with an elasticity in terms of income of over 2 per cent, grew, in the long term, much more quickly than manufacturing (see Table 1.4). Commercial services performed more or less proportionally to gross domestic product while all other services rose more slowly than the latter. The sector's overall performance depended on the opposing tendencies of services with high productivity gains and income elasticity and services whose importance was gradually disappearing in the course of modern economic growth; a typical case being that of personal and domestic service.

The division into sub-periods as seen in Table 1.4 is less detailed than that of the previous two tables: cyclical swings in the service sector are less pronounced than those in the industrial sector. This is due both to the relative stability of their demand and to the methods adopted in estimating their output. Value added by the tertiary sector is estimated from indicators which are directly or indirectly linked to its employment (which, in the short term, tended to remain fairly stable despite variations in demand). Given the rough approximation of these estimates, it is possible only to observe the trend acceleration which took place, in this sector too, after 1896. This should come as no surprise since increases in activity in other sectors typically lead to an increase in demand for transport, banking services, and commercial intermediation.

The civil service sector performed similarly: its value added is conventionally measured as the sum of salaries paid to state employees, deflated with the retail price index or the cost of living. Until 1909 the share of this sector in gross domestic product remained essentially unvaried at around 5 per cent. Government services grew by an average of 0.8 per cent per annum until 1896 and by 2.4 per cent until 1909. It was only from 1910 onwards, starting with preparations for the war against the Ottoman Empire, that the sector grew at far higher rates than those of national income: 5.7 per cent between 1909 and 1913, followed by a very rapid expansion. In 1918, the sector's value added reached 30 per cent of gross domestic product. The drastic reduction in public expenditure which followed did not manage to bring the sector back to the relative level of the period 1861–1909: in 1925 this represented around 6.5 per cent of Italy's national income. The

Table 1.4 The production of services in Italy 1861–1925 (average annual growth rates at constant prices)

Period	Transport and communications	Credit and insurance	Trade	Miscellaneous services	Building rents	Total services	Public administration
1861–1925	3.9	6.1	1.4	0.7	0.8	1.2	1.8
1861–96	3.2	7.9	0.6	0.6	0.8	0.9	0.8
1896–1913	8.0	4.3	2.2	1.4	1.1	1.7	3.1
1913–25	0.0	3.2	2.4	0.0	0.6	1.2	2.8

Source: As for Table 1.3.

'great depression' of the early 1930s and, especially, the war in Ethiopia would once again considerably widen the Italian public sector.

Chapter two

Demand

Demand in modern economic growth

The increase in time of per capita income, characteristic of
Kuznets' modern economic growth, is accompanied by considerable changes in the composition of demand. 'Engel's Law'
consists in the empirical observation that a rise in income leads to a
less than proportional increase in the amount spent on foodstuffs.
This 'law' may be generalized by observing that it is possible to
rank the various consumer goods according to their income
elasticity of demand. Individuals and societies alike tend first of all
to satisfy the primary needs of food, clothing, and housing. Above
the basic subsistence level, as income rises, there is a more than
proportional growth in demand for transport, education, and
entertainment, while an increasing part of income goes in savings.
In each society this general 'law' governing the pattern of
expenditure acquires particular features due to factors such as
income distribution, climate, culture, and whether or not there
exists a tradition of state intervention. Kuznets' modern economic
growth is, typically, accompanied by an increase in the ratio of
investment to national income from the 5 to 6 per cent typical of
traditional economies up to the level of 15 to 20 per cent characterizing developed economic systems. Savings follow more or less
the same pattern; however it should be noted that often domestic
savings are not sufficient, especially in the early stages of modern
economic growth, to finance investment demand completely. This
gap can be filled by foreign savings.

Until 1914 modern economic growth was characterized by
growing international specialization and by a tendency towards
market integration both of goods and of factors of production.
Therefore, international trade grew faster than world income: an
increasing part of each country's demand was made up of imports
and exports. The First World War abruptly interrupted this process

Table 2.1 Composition of Italy's aggregate demand 1861–1925

Year	Private consumption %	Public consumption %	Gross investments %	Exports %	Total %
1861	80.9	7.6	5.3	6.2	100.00
1876	77.0	6.4	4.7	11.9	100.00
1888	72.9	6.5	10.6	10.0	100.00
1896	74.8	7.0	7.1	11.1	100.00
1908	69.6	5.6	12.9	11.9	100.00
1913	65.4	7.1	15.1	12.4	100.00
1925	63.8	8.3	15.6	12.3	100.00

Source: P. Ercolani, 'Documentazione statistica di base', in G. Fuà (ed.), *Lo sviluppo economico in Italia*, Milan: Angeli, 1969, vol. III, pp. 422–3.

of international economic integration, which was to revive only from the 1950s onwards.

These general tendencies can also be observed in the Italian case between 1861 and 1925 and are summarized in Table 2.1. In 1861, 81 per cent of the Italians' income went on private consumption – a very high value, typical of a backward country. The amount of investment was correspondingly low. In the decades that followed, there was a steady fall in the proportion of resources devoted to private consumption and an overall stability, until 1913, of public consumption. The ratio of investment to national income, cyclically highly unstable, in the long run seemed to follow the path of Italian economic growth and was characterized by a trend acceleration from the mid-1890s onward.

Consumption

Between 1861 and 1896 the growth rate in private consumption was slightly lower than that of the population. Going by existing data, therefore, per capita consumption in Italy would remain unchanged for more than a generation after the country's political unification. It should be noted, however, that welfare, consumption and standards of living have not received by Italian historians the attention rightly given them in other countries: the current view that private consumption per capita did not increase during 1861–96 must, therefore, be confirmed by further research. It is nevertheless consistent with the observed lack of political consensus of the great mass of citizens, particularly in the poor South, for the unified political entity that emerged from the Risorgimento, and with the difficulty with which law and order were maintained in Italy during the second half of the nineteeth century.[1] Welfare will be discussed further in Chapter four.

The structure of demand of consumer goods changed very slowly in the post-Unification period. Expenditure on food fell from about 70 per cent of the total in the first twenty years after Unification to 63 per cent in 1919. Expenditure on clothing remained stable at around 10 per cent. The figure for housing (subject to a higher margin of error) tended to fall, while that for other high income elasticity items slowly increased. The overall tendency reflects the main features of the process of modern economic growth as described by Kuznets: the Italian case, however, was characterized by an extreme slowness in the structural changes of private consumption (see Table 2.2).

Table 2.2 Indices of per capita income and consumption (1861 = 100)

Year	Per capita GDP	Total private consumption per capita	Per capita consumption in			
			Food	Clothing	Housing	Other goods
1861	100	100	100	100	100	100
1876	103	102	104	95	82	132
1888	101	95	94	89	85	143
1896	101	103	92	102	84	257
1908	132	118	112	80	90	285
1913	145	121	112	103	91	311
1919	155	123	120	101	91	257
1922	145	132	128	126	91	284
1925	163	138	126	165	92	337

Source: P. Ercolani, 'Documentazione statistica di base', op. cit., pp. 424–30.

The stagnation, which according to the available estimates, characterized the period 1861–96, was reflected in the overall pattern of per capita consumption. It is interesting to see that consumption was low during the investment boom of the 1880s and that it increased slightly during the ensuing contraction in investment demand. On the whole, however, even taking into account the considerable margin of statistical error, it would appear that the average Italian's consumption, during the mid-1890s, was no higher than that of his father in about 1860.

Food consumption seems actually to have fallen by 8 per cent. It may be argued that the 1861 levels of both gross product and consumption have been overestimated (the figure for housing is especially suspect) but it is unlikely that a revision downward would make any significant difference to the impression gained from Table 2.2. This is an important point for an understanding of

Italy's history as a whole. Whatever may ultimately emerge from the ongoing revision of the series of statistics for industrial production, a growth rate of the latter much higher than that estimated by ISTAT would not have a significant impact on current estimates of per capita consumption for the period 1860–90, given Italy's narrow industrial base at the time of the Unification. The argument that the level of food consumption might be underestimated given the difficulty in accounting for auto-consumption (that is, goods consumed directly by the producers) is not sufficient for holding that the rate of growth in such consumption was significantly different from that described in Table 2.2. This index may, therefore, be read as a synthesis, more significant than others, of the disappointment soon felt by the *petite bourgeoisie* and the middle class which had fought the wars of independence and, above all, of the lack of interest on the part of the masses in the new state. If one remembers the difference in income between north and south, it is not difficult to understand, when reading Table 2.2, some of the important reasons for keeping 300,000 soldiers stationed in the territories of the ex-Kingdom of the Two Sicilies.

The 'boom' of the Giolitti years saw an increase in per capita private consumption (at an average annual rate of around 1 per cent between 1896 and 1913). The difference between the increase in income and that in consumption, however, was high and accounts for the strong accumulation rate characterizing that period. At any rate, it was only after 1896 that the average Italian significantly increased his food consumption. The trend continued with the First World War: in this case, the aggregate datum probably hides the different treatment given to fighting troops and to urban populations, while the mass of peasants remaining in rural areas had to rely mainly on auto-consumption.

Investment

As we have already seen (Table 2.1), gross investment started from a very low level, accelerated for the first time during the 1880s, experienced a sharp fall during the following slump, and then began a long wave of expansion right up to the First World War.

The best estimate of the stock of capital and gross investment remains that made by Ornello Vitali for the Fuà group.[2] The theoretical problems connected with the comparison of the value of various investments in different periods are such that many economists maintain that this exercise is founded on extremely weak logical bases.[3] The figures referred to here should be seen at best as rough orders of magnitude, despite the apparent precision

Table 2.3 Indices of investment in Italy 1861–1925 (1861 = 100)

| Period | GDP | Total gross investment | Gross investment in machinery, industrial equipment and transport | Net investments in public works | |
				Vitali	Fenoaltea
1861–3	100	100	100	100	100
1875–7	111	109	135	62	75
1887–9	119	203	307	166	147
1895–7	126	132	240	79	60
1907–9	181	477	885	84	138
1911–13	208	502	963	130	200
1924–6	239	616	1285	—	—

Source: O. Vitali, 'La stima degli investimenti e dello stock di capitale', in G. Fuà (ed.), op. cit., pp. 478–537.

Note: All variables are at 1938 prices.

with which they are presented. It should also be added that investments fluctuated considerably in the short term: this long-term trend is therefore particularly sensitive to the choice of the base and end years.

In the long run, total gross investment rose at a rate which was approximately double that of domestic product. Gross expenditure in machinery and equipment rose at an average annual rate of more than 8 per cent: almost four times that of GDP. Overall, Table 2.3 shows an important accumulation process which appears, at least in arithmetical terms, understandable if considered in the light of what has been said about consumption patterns. Gross investments were characterized by very pronounced cyclical upswings that are not entirely described by Table 2.3. The period when the Right was in power (1861–76) seems characterized by stagnation in gross investment and by moderate growth in machinery and equipment. Under the Left there was a fairly strong cyclical upswing with average annual growth rates of 5.3 and 7.1 per cent for the two series. The turning points were between 1887 and 1888. The 1890s were characterized by a long interruption in the accumulation process: only between 1899 and 1900 would investment in machinery and equipment once again reach the 1887–8 level.

Between 1900 and 1907 aggregate gross investment grew at the incredible annual rate of about 10 per cent. The following six years showed strong fluctuations around an essentially stationary trend. During the First World War the increase in the stock of capital remained negligible.

These trends, together with those in industrial production, have in the past given rise to lively discussions as to the moment in which modern economic growth could be said to have begun in Italy. A summary of the various opinions on this subject is given in Chapter twelve, but it is useful now to dispel any error in the interpretation of existing data. Since investments are subject to pronounced cyclical fluctuations, some authors have dated the beginning of 'growth' from the beginning of each cyclical phase, arguing that from then on an essentially uninterrupted accumulation process took place. In fact, from the mid-1870s on, growth in investment seemed to show periods of very rapid expansion followed by long phases of recession or slump, each cycle lasting some ten years.

Any analysis, however summary, of investment patterns is not complete without taking into account the recent, meticulous estimates of public works produced by Fenoaltea[4] which differ sharply from the preceding ones. Public expenditure on social over-head capital showed a highly pro-cyclical profile. Moreover, Fenoaltea's estimates show a greater rate of growth in investment during the Giolitti era than do those of Vitali.

Public expenditure

The essential stability of the share of public consumption in gross domestic product is mirrored in the similar pattern of public expenditure which, for the central government, can be estimated at about 11 per cent of the national income both in 1861 and in 1910.[5] There were, however, fluctuations during this period. The war of 1866 provoked a real increase in public expenditure of about 43 per cent. This jump did not produce a 'ratchet-effect': until 1880 government spending fluctuated again around 11 per cent of national income, with a slight increase due to military expenses in 1870. Between 1880 and 1889, the growth rate in real terms of public spending was 6.3 per cent per annum: in this case, too, defence explains most of the increase. In the twenty years that followed, the share of government spending in national income fell slowly from 18 to 10 per cent. It rose again sharply during the Great War, reaching 59 per cent in 1918.

The structure of government spending is summarized in Table 2.4. Three-quarters to over four-fifths of total public spending in peace time was devoted by Liberal Italy to defence and to debt service. Military spending until 1896 amounted to about 4 per cent of national income. During the 'Age of the Right' (about 1861–76) this amount of resources was very close to that taken by gross investment, and until the beginning of the Giolitti era it was about half of the latter. In 1908, defence accounted for only 2 per cent of government spending; but it rose again to 5 per cent in 1913.

Table 2.4 Composition of Italy's public expenditure

Year	Interest on debt and general administration	Defence	Justice and police	Transfers to the economy	Other
1862	37.2	39.1	3.0	17.0	3.7
1876	62.5	20.3	2.3	12.4	2.5
1888	54.4	27.4	2.0	14.6	1.6
1896	58.2	25.8	1.9	11.5	2.6
1908	52.4	22.7	2.1	20.6	2.2
1913	39.7	35.9	1.6	18.5	4.3
1919	11.6	82.7	1.1	3.0	1.6
1925	38.9	31.0	5.9	14.6	9.6

Source: P. Ercolani, 'Documentazione statistica di base', op. cit., pp. 436–7.

Interest payments depended on the deficits accumulated in previous periods. The years from 1862 to 1874 were characterized by high public deficit: at its peak, during the war of 1866, this reached 8 per cent of national income and, excluding that year, the average for the decade was about 4 per cent. Around 1875 the Right nearly managed to balance the budget and deficits remained modest for the following ten years. They rose again to high levels from 1886 to 1893. After 1899 a balanced budget policy was followed (in 1907 the surplus was 1 per cent of national income) but in 1913 expenditure was once again well below revenue. There then followed the great war-time deficit spending: inflation was instrumental, however, in reducing the stock of debt accumulated and thus the resources absorbed by the payment of interest were, relative to GDP, lower in 1925 than in 1896.

Foreign accounts

Strictly speaking this chapter should deal only with foreign demand. However, it is useful to consider briefly the whole issue of Italy's balance of payments. In a relatively backward country, without raw materials, 'import capacity' becomes one of the key variables in modern economic growth. This capacity depends both on the exports of goods in which the backward country has a comparative advantage (usually highly labour-intensive goods) and on capital imports.

Table 2.5 shows deficits and surpluses of the trade and current account balances. Italy was definitely characterized, in what may be defined as a 'structural' way, by an almost permanent trade deficit: only between 1872 and 1882 would there be a substantial

Table 2.5 Balances of trade and current account (deficits and surpluses as % of GDP)

Average for years	Balance or trade	Balance of payments on current account
1861−3	−3.1	−3.3
1875−7	−1.1	−0.3
1887−9	−3.4	−2.5
1895−7	−0.5	+1.9
1907−9	−5.6	−1.1
1911−13	−5.0	0.0
1919−21	−10.6	−8.2
1924−6	−4.4	−1.2

Source: P. Ercolani, 'Documentazione statistica di base', op. cit., pp. 453−4.
Note: The − sign indicates a deficit, the + sign a surplus.

equilibrium in the balance of trade.[6] Deficits were smaller than average also between 1894 and 1899. Overall, it may be noted how they increased in periods of expansion of production and investments in the manufacturing sector: the 1880s and the Giolitti era. Such a pattern is typical of the first phases of modern economic growth.

The balance of payments on the current account showed, in the years under consideration, deficits far lower than those in the balance of trade. In the first decade after political unification the balance of trade deficit was only partly compensated by other current account transactions and was, therefore, financed by foreign debt, the stock of which, by the end of the period, may be estimated to have been about a quarter of the national product.

Table 2.6 Outstanding foreign debt

Period ending	Outstanding foreign debt	
	% GDP (1)	Debt divided by revenue from foreign transactions (2)
1870	24.9	2.4
1883	18.9	1.3
1890	31.6	2.6
1893	31.8	2.3
1907	−13.0	−0.7
1913	−9.1	−0.5

Source: See Table 2.5

Note: In columns (1) and (2) the − sign indicates net foreign credit.

In the following decade, the improvement in the balance of trade made it possible to reduce the outstanding foreign debt. This increased again considerably during the 1880s when the strong growth in imports was only partially compensated by the revenue from services and factors of production (see Table 2.6); hence a new inflow of foreign capital.

From 1890 on, the overall structure of Italian foreign accounts underwent a considerable transformation. Until that time, the capacity to finance trade deficits created by the cyclical expansion in investments depended by about two-thirds on the possibility of importing capital from abroad. After 1890, and particularly during the Giolitti era, Italy's import capacity was no longer determined by the availability of international capital. Tourism and emigrants' remittances not only succeeded in financing the growing demand for imports but are likely to have produced, by 1913, a modest net credit position abroad. This was swept away during the early months of the First World War. In 1920 the foreign debt accumulated by Italy was equal to half the national product.

Chapter three

The financial superstructure

Modern economic growth and financial intermediation

No discussion of the development of a modern economy is possible
without reference to the evolution of its financial system which
undergoes a 'modernization' process similar to that of real side of
the economy and which, in its turn, influences growth and the
characteristics thereof.

It is easy to make the general statement that, in a world in which
savers and investors are separate entities, the diffusion of financial
instruments is a necessary condition for real investment. It is not
easy, however, to proceed from this broad statement to an evaluation of the contribution that a particular organization (quantitative
and qualitative) of the so-called financial superstructure may give
to the growth in the quantity of goods and services produced by an
economic system. Theory and empirical investigation on this point
have somehow lagged behind in the progress of development
economics. Historical research is therefore limited in this field by
constraints on the theory side: it may, none the less, proceed to
describe some important phenomena and advance hypotheses that
may, in due time, catch the eye of the theoretical economist.[1] The
frame of reference for the following account of the long-term
evolution of Italy's financial intermediation system is obviously
based upon the work of Raymond Goldsmith,[2] in which the
performance of the main financial variables is studied with an
approach and methods not that dissimilar to Kuznets'.

According to Goldsmith,

the relation between a country's financial superstructure and its
real infrastructure is reflected in the financial interrelation ratio
(FIR). The ratio is obtained by dividing the total (partly dupli-
cated) value of all financial assets in existence at one date by the
total value of tangible assets plus net foreign balance, i.e. by
national wealth.[3]

The financial superstructures of individual countries differ one from the other owing both to previous history and to the epoch in which modern growth began. Successive development takes place at different times and at different speeds, and is related also to the overall performance of the real variables, but, according to Goldsmith,

> the evidence now available is more in favour of the hypothesis that there exists only one major path of financial development, a path marked by certain regularities in the course of the financial interrelation ratio, in the share of financial institutions in total financial assets, and in the position of the banking system.[4]

In the course of modern economic growth the 'financial superstructure' grows more rapidly than the 'structure' constituted by real income and wealth. Therefore the FIR, whose initial values are very low, tends to rise to a value somewhere between 1 and 1.5 beyond which it tends to stabilize. Real growth is usually accompanied by a growing specialization and separation of the savings and investment processes. This is reflected in an increase in the issues by non-financial sectors, of foreign issues and of issues of financial institutions to gross national product (ANIR or Aggregate New Issue Ratio).

The main regularities in the evolution of the financial intermediation system during modern economic growth are the following: (a) there is first a rise and then a fall in the ratio of currency (banknotes and metal coins) to national income; (b) the same pattern, though not synchronous with the former, is observed in the ratio of bank money (sight deposits) to national income; (c) the share of financial institutions in the issuance and the ownership of financial assets increases considerably (a process sometimes called 'institutionalization of savings'); (d) the share of the banking system in the assets of all financial institutions declines; (e) the cost of financing tends to diminish; and (f) as real income and wealth increase so do the size and complexity of the financial superstructure.

Financial intermediation and development in Italy

The most reliable time series for a study of the Italian banking intermediation system are those edited by Renato de Mattia.[5] Estimates of the overall amount of financial assets and national wealth are scanty: reliable estimates of FIR exist only for few years and show a growth from 0.38 in 1881 to 0.47 in 1914.[6] These values are only slightly higher than half of those observed on average in five developed countries during the same years.[7] In Italy as in most other cases therefore, a relative backwardness in terms of per capita income was accompanied by a similar backwardness in the financial superstructure. The other characteristics of the latter's evolution would tend to confirm this conclusion. The ratio between money in circulation and GDP diminished very slowly from 21 per cent in 1882 to 17 per cent in 1924. The growth of bank deposits was fairly rapid: in 1882 these equalled only 14 per cent of gross national income, reached a level of 37 per cent in 1905, remained at more or less the same level for the following ten years, fell during the First World War, and rose again to 37 per cent in 1925. The time path of this variable, is only in part connected with Italy's backwardness: one of the country's peculiar features is, in fact, the greater than average importance of the banks in the financial structure, a feature common to other 'latecomers' (such as Germany and Japan) during the early phases of modern economic growth. Further confirmation of this peculiarity can be seen in the fact that the liabilities of the banking system, which in 1870 were 97.8 per cent of the total liabilities of financial intermediaries, remained at about the same level until 1925.

Table 3.1 shows in some detail the cyclical behaviour of the liabilities of financial intermediaries. Small variations apart, two rapid expansion phases in financial intermediation can be detected, both coinciding with a strong cyclical growth in industrial output: the 1880s and the 1920s. In these two phases financial intermediaries played an important role in accelerating the re-allocation of resources to those sectors where demand was particularly dynamic.

The characteristics and the very size of the crises which followed these phases of industrial and financial growth also depended on the role played by intermediaries during these periods of expansion. The slow growth of the financial superstructure between 1887 and 1896 is evident: the prolonged slump in production referred to in previous chapters was accompanied by a serious banking crisis which culminated in the failure of important banks and in the creation of the Bank of Italy (1893). The effects of these events may be observed in columns 2 and 4 of Table 3.1.

The relationship between finance and growth during the Giolitti era was more complex. In aggregate terms, the growth in the intermediaries' liabilities seems modest especially if one considers its real income elasticity – the lowest among those of all the sub-periods examined, including the depression of the 1890s.[8]

As Biscaini and Ciocca have rightly pointed out, there is no confirmation 'on a merely quantitative ground, of the hypothesis that

Table 3.1 Evolution of the financial superstructure

		Liabilities of financial intermediaries			
	Average growth rate p.a. (1)	Total banking system (2)	Banks of issue (3)	Commercial banks (4)	Leading 'mixed banks' (5)
1870	—	97.9	66.6	10.9	—
1877	3.9	93.7	39.4	27.8	—
1887	8.7	90.2	27.2	23.3	—
1896	1.8	85.5	26.2	10.4	1.7
1913	3.5	89.9	18.5	19.3	15.4
1920	—	95.8	32.0	29.9	27.0
1925	6.4	92.8	23.2	33.1	16.6
1870–1925	4.0	—	—	—	—

Source: A.M. Biscaini Cotula and P.L. Ciocca, 'Le strutture finanziarie: aspetti quantitativi di lungo periodo (1870–1970)', in F. Vicarelli (ed.), Capitale industriale e capitale finanziario: il caso italiano, Bologna: Il Mulino, 1979.

Notes: Column (1): values at 1938 constant prices; column (4): Banca commerciale Italiana, Credito Italiano, Banco di Roma, Società Bancaria Italiana (until 1914), and Banca Italiana di Sconto (1914–20). In 1925 the first three banks only.

in the first Italian "take-off", given the "forced" nature of the process, the overall role of finance – regardless of changes in its composition – was more important than in other periods'.[9] It should also be pointed out that during these years 'resort by firms to external finance was minimal'.[10] It is, therefore, in the qualitative changes of the intermediation system that one should look for a possible link between finance and real growth during the Giolitti era. While the relative importance of the banking system remained unaltered between 1887 and 1914 its composition changed. Between 1896 and 1913 the importance of the banks of issue declined, while that of the commercial banks rose (see Table 3.1). However, the share of the latter in the total liabilities of the system was, in 1913, still below the 1875 and 1887 levels. What could be considered new in this period was the growth of the leading 'mixed' (or 'universal') banks and it is to their growth that Gerschenkron's interpretation of Italy's industrial 'take-off' is linked (see Chapter twelve).

Chapter four

Production, productivity, and welfare

Population and labour input

The long-term growth of gross product depends on the increase in inputs – labour, land, and capital – and on technical progress, broadly defined to include organization, managerial skills, the opening of new markets, economies of scale, and the like.

The measurement of input implies practical and theoretical difficulties which are probably greater than those faced when estimating production.[1] The heterogeneity of labour and capital, the fact that the services given by both are distributed over variable and unknown periods of time, and the process of 'learning by doing' are only a few of the most obvious circumstances which make many scholars sceptical as to the validity of measures leading to estimate aggregate production functions. This scepticism increases when one considers the theoretical implications of such empirical methods. The use of market prices as indicators of the value of the resources used in production – the only way of arriving at a homogeneous evaluation of inputs – is possible only under the strict hypotheses within which neo-classical theory equates value and price. In particular, it is not easy to assume that an underdeveloped economy of the nineteenth century would be characterized by perfect competition and by full employment of resources. Moreover, the conditions prevailing during the transition from a 'traditional' underdeveloped society to one characterized by modern economic growth do not seem to be the most appropriate for an empirical description of 'economic equilibrium'.

Although aware of these problems, scholars have tried to quantify the pattern and contribution of individual factors of production in the growth of output. According to Kuznets, 'the scanty available data suggest that increase in inputs per head of man-hours and material capital combined accounted for less than a fifth of the secular rise in production per capita';[2] in fact 'the

25

epochal innovation which distinguishes the modern economic epoch is the extended application of science to the problems of economic production.'[3]

As far as labour is concerned, it may be said, in general, that, from a secular perspective, the large increase in population which characterizes modern economic growth has little or no effect on increases in inputs of work-hours in the productive process since growth itself is associated with a conspicuous fall in the number of hours worked during the year (reductions in the number of working hours per week, longer annual holidays and paid sick-leave) and in the course of each person's working life (later entry into and earlier retirement from the labour market). At the same time, the share of the labour force in population tends to increase in almost all countries during the early phases of modern economic growth: from this point of view, Italy is one of the few exceptions pointed out by Kuznets.[4]

A brief analysis of the patterns in labour inputs in the period 1861–1921 might usefully begin with a look at demographic changes. These are summarized in Table 4.1.

Table 4.1 Demographic variables 1861–1920

Period	Growth rate of population	Births	Deaths	Natural growth	Net migration
1861–70	6.2	37.6	30.3	7.3	1.1
1871–80	5.1	36.9	29.9	7.0	1.9
1881–90	6.9	37.8	27.3	10.5	3.6
1891–1900	5.4	35.0	24.2	10.8	5.4
1901–10	6.8	32.7	21.6	11.1	4.3
1911–20	2.3	27.2	20.6	6.6	4.3

Source: ISTAT, *Sommario di statistiche storiche*, Rome, 1968, pp. 12 *et seq.*

Note: Growth rates are annual averages per 1,000. The other values are ratios per 1,000 inhabitants.

The natural increase in population tended to rise until the Great War as a result of slightly declining birth rates, at least from the 1880s onwards, and of a much more striking fall in mortality rates. The total growth of the population was gradually contained by a rise in emigration.

Compared with the leading European countries (Table 4.2), Italy, at the moment of political unification, had a high mortality rate, a fact which confirms the backwardness of the country (this variable is known to be influenced by per capita income levels). In the first sixty years after Unification, Italy's mortality rate fell

Table 4.2 Birth and death rates per 1,000 inhabitants in some European countries, 1861 and 1913

Country	1861		1913	
	Births	*Deaths*	*Births*	*Deaths*
Sweden	32.6	18.5	23.2	13.7
UK	34.6	21.6	24.1	13.8
France	26.9	23.2	18.8	17.7
Low Countries	33.0	23.9	28.2	12.3
Germany	35.7	25.6	27.5	15.0
Spain	39.0	26.6	30.6	22.3
Austria	37.4	29.8	29.7	20.3
Italy	38.0	30.9	31.7	18.7
Russia	49.7	35.4	43.1	27.4

Source: B.R. Mitchell, *European Historical Statistics*, London: Macmillan, 1978, pp. 20–31.

steadily: just before the First World War it was more than 30 per cent lower than it had been in 1861 (in 1970 it was around 9.7 per thousand). By 1913 the gap between Italy and countries with higher per capita incomes had narrowed. The natural growth rate of the population, which fell in most other countries, rose considerably in Italy owing to a smaller reduction in birth rates than elsewhere.

Labour inputs are much more difficult to estimate from Italian population censuses and one must rely entirely on Vitali's patient work which has produced the only available estimates of Italy's labour force.[5] Using these data, Fuà[6] has calculated the sectorial and total growth rates of the Italian labour force, which are summarized in Table 4.3.

Labour inputs increased at a rate which was about half that of the population throughout the period from the Unification to the

Table 4.3 Growth rates of employment (per 1,000)

Sectors	1881–97	1897–1913	1913–21
Agriculture	8	−3	13
Industry	−9	16	−9
Services	2	12	8
Total employment	3	3	7
Population	7	6	4

Source: G. Fuà, *Formazione, distribuzione e impiego del reddito dal 1861: sintesi statistica*, Rome: ISCO, 1972, Table 2.9.

War. The fall in the activity rate – that is, the ratio of workers to total resident population – which dropped from 56 to 50 per cent during 1881–1911 was mainly due to a fall in the number of women in the labour force. There was no reduction, however, in the same period of time, in the percentage in the labour force of males under fifteen or over sixty-five years of age.[7]

Table 4.3 shows only the number of workers employed in the production process: a precise estimate of labour inputs would require the transformation into homogeneous units of types of labour quite different in their efficiency (due, for example, to disparities in the physical strength of men, women, children, and the old, or to varying degrees of education or skill). It is easy to understand the complexity of these kinds of estimates and as yet they have not been attempted by Italian economic historians. The fact that the reduction in the female labour force 'explained' almost entirely the fall in the activity rate might indicate that, in terms of units of comparable efficiency, labour inputs grew more rapidly than would appear from Table 4.3. This phenomenon might have been strengthened by a higher level of education among workers, although scholars are not sure that this leads to increased efficiency in the type of occupations prevailing during the early phases of modern economic growth. Hypotheses concerning the hours worked by each person in the course of the year are also quite risky. It is likely that in agriculture and in some manufacturing sectors facing an excess supply of labour the average amount of work done by each person during the year remained more or less constant, below full employment, and therefore unaffected by changes in the legal and actual length of the working day.[8]

Finally, one should note the sectorial patterns of labour inputs described in Table 4.3: going by the census data alone the number of those active in the industrial sector would appear to have diminished considerably during the first thirty or forty years after the Unification. Were it to find confirmation, this phenomenon would certainly be interesting and peculiar to Italy: there are, however, good reasons for believing that the estimates made in 1861 and 1871 are highly unreliable as regards the assignment of workers engaged both in agriculture and in cottage industry to one or other of the two sectors, with a likely overestimate of the latter in 1861.[9]

In conclusion, it can be said that the beginning of modern economic growth took place, as in most analogous historical experiences, in the context or increases in the natural growth rates of population due to a more rapid fall in mortality than in birthrates. Due to emigration, the annual increase of the population actually present in the country remained more or less stable throughout the period under consideration. In the long term, the labour force grew by three thousand each year, but the economic significance of this figure remains very rough because of the already mentioned difficulty in estimating labour input (hours, days) of homogeneous efficiency.

Product per worker and per unit of capital

According to Fuà, total aggregate product per worker grew slowly until 1897 and then rose sharply, in part owing to the increase that took place in the agricultural sector. Much more contained, although important, was the acceleration in the industrial and service sectors.

Table 4.4 Gross product per worker and net product per unit of fixed capital (annual growth rates %*)

Sectors	1881–97		1897–1913		1913–21	
	Labour %	Capital %	Labour %	Capital %	Labour %	Capital %
Agriculture	−0.7	..	2.2	2.0	−1.6	..
Industry	1.6		2.6		0.9	
		−1.3		..		..
Services	1.2		2.5		1.5	
Total	0.3	−0.2	2.4	1.4	..	..

Source: Our estimates from G. Fuà, *Formazione, distribuzione e impiego del reddito dal 1861: sintesi statistica*, Rome: ISCO, 1972, Tables 5.1, 5.15.

Notes: *Excluding housing and public works; a. .. indicates values close to zero.

Bearing in mind the way in which the data have been estimated in Table 4.4, it is easy to see how the agrarian crisis, accompanied by an increase in the number of workers in the sector, generated the fall in product per worker between 1881 and 1897, and how the increase in production and the transfer of labour to other sectors produced the opposite result during the Giolitti years. It must be added that, according to Fuà,[10] most of the increase in product per worker in agriculture in the period 1897–1913 is not explained by reductions in the labour force: the reawakening of Italian agriculture in the years before the Great War was, in effect, characterized by a series of technical and organizational innovations of great importance, the effects of which find striking parallels in these simple calculations. In Table 4.5 the level and growth in Italian product per man-hour are compared with those in other countries.

Table 4.5   Level and growth rates of GDP per man-hour

Country	Product per man-hour*			Growth rates**	
	1880	1900	1913	1880–1900	1900–13
France	0.53	0.71	0.90	1.47	1.84
Germany	0.50	0.79	0.95	2.31	1.43
Sweden	0.37	0.59	0.83	2.36	2.66
United Kingdom	0.94	1.20	1.35	1.23	0.91
United States	0.88	1.29	1.67	1.93	2.00
Italy	0.45	0.53	0.72	0.82	2.35

Source: A. Maddison, *Phases of Capitalist Development*, Oxford: Oxford University Press, 1983, p. 212.
Notes: * In 1970 USA dollars; ** average annual percentage.

The level of product per man-hour in Italy does not seem exceptionally low when compared with that in other countries (the analogous value around 1880 in Japan was around 0.20), while what is striking is the modest level of growth realized until 1900. The low rate of growth in product and productivity before the end of the century raises problems of interpretation which will be discussed in Chapter twelve. During the Giolitti years, on the contrary, product per man-hour grew, in Italy, at a rate which was among the highest in Europe.

Table 4.6   Net product per lira of fixed capital*

Sector	1881	1897	1913	1921	1949	1967
Agriculture	0.13	0.13	0.18	0.18	0.17	0.22
Industry and services	0.48	0.36	0.35	0.35	0.50	0.76
Total	0.20	0.20	0.25	0.26	0.30	0.56

Source: G. Fuà, *Formazione, distribuzione e impiego del reddito dal 1861: Sintesi statistica*, Rome: ISCO, 1972, Table 5.15.
Note: * Excluding housing and public works.

Table 4.6 contains estimates of net product per unit of fixed capital. These are, as has already been said, much more risky estimates than those, however approximate, relating to labour productivity: they represent, however, the best 'guesses' available at present. The low capital/product ratio in agriculture comes as no surprise given the relatively high value of land, a scarce factor in Italy. As far as industry and services are concerned, the fall in net product per unit of capital in 1891–7 may be due to the fact that investments in social overhead capital and large enterprises had rather low or deferred profitability. The fact that the net product of capital did not grow in the Giolitti years is more difficult to explain: again one might argue that investment in capital intensive sectors in which, at the time, Italy did not have a comparative advantage, did not maximize returns in the short run.

Unfortunately, it is impossible to complete this summary with estimates of total factor productivity since both the necessary data and econometric analyses are lacking in Italy. This is regrettable since, in the case of other countries, the research necessary for the construction of solid aggregate and sectorial production functions have contributed considerably to quantitative history by creating veritable goldmines of data which have been used for various purposes. There is, however, less cause to regret the absence of actual econometric estimates of aggregate production functions: the underlying theory does not provide one of the best tools for economic historians.

A highly approximate indication of the growth in net product per unit of productive factors may, however, be obtained from Fuà's estimates[11] according to which it was near zero for the economy as a whole from 1881–97 and subsequently rose rapidly (2.4 per cent a year) during the Giolitti years.

Conditions of life and welfare

Those who have grown up in the material and intellectual climate of the West during the last forty years will find it difficult to understand that only very recently has the final aim of modern economic growth been seen as the promotion of welfare for each citizen. Not that long ago, growth in national income was pursued more often than not for very different reasons: in particular, it was oriented towards maximizing the power, not necessarily only military, of the sovereign and of the ruling classes. This applied particularly in the case of the mercantilist policies on which the economic philosophy of the great nation–states was based in the seventeenth and eighteenth centuries. It is not necessary, however, to go back two centuries or indeed leave Italy in order to find other similar examples: Mussolini's ideal of producing and supporting 'eight million soldiers' indicates nothing other than a subordination of the economy and of demography itself to the 'ethical' ends of state power. Nor does today's world lack examples, more or less explicit, of countries and areas where the pursual of individual welfare is not the primary objective of economic growth. While our purpose here is not the discussion of what may have been the ultimate economic objectives of the ruling class during the Risorgimento, nor, indeed, of those leading the country's governments, a brief mention of this question serves as a reminder that the scarcity of *systematic* statistics for the average Italian's living conditions and, above all, for those of the working classes, should not surprise the reader.

It goes without saying that, even were the best possible indicators available, the choice of those best suited for the measurement of the 'welfare' of a population or class is conditioned by the underlying value judgements of the scholars attempting to define and measure welfare itself. The debate on the living conditions of the working class during the Industrial Revolution in England is so shot through with value judgements that the contending factions have been divided into 'optimists' and 'pessimists'. While the former emphasize the increase in real wages which took place after the French wars, the latter throw the argument back in their faces by indicating how this increase was often spent on gin, at the time a real drug for the poor. In fact, the increase in alcohol consumption may also be seen, according to individual value judgements, as an index of increased or decreased welfare. This should be taken into account in evaluating the quantitative considerations which follow.

In the second half of the nineteenth century Italy was certainly one of the poorest countries in Europe. The gap between her per capita income and that of the most advanced Continental countries, however, was not enormous: in 1870 Italian per capita income was perhaps about 80 per cent that of Germany and France (and it was about half that of the richest country, the United Kingdom).[12] This gap widened until the end of the century. Per capita income is only one, and not necessarily the best, of the possible indicators of welfare.

The most obvious alternative way of measuring welfare in a poor society starting out on the road towards modern economic growth consists in estimating the per capita availability of foodstuffs and their composition, taking into account that food constituted on average 68.6 per cent of Italian private consumption in the years 1874–93 and 65.6 per cent in the period 1894–1913.[13] Table 4.7 shows the average availability in quantity and quality of the main sources of nutrition as well as the estimated number of calories consumed per person.

Going by these figures, the average Italian would seem to have been sufficiently well-nourished, if one takes into account that only part of the population was composed of male adult manual workers. There was, however, an imbalance in the composition of the diet: about 80 per cent of it being of vegetable origin.[14] The problem posed is clearly one of distribution: given that the average

Table 4.7 Daily per capita availability of nutrients and calories

	Protein	Fats	Carbohydrates	Calories
1874–93[1]	78.48	61.23	362.01	2,363
1894–1913[1]	85.04	58.79	388.12	2,475
Normal requirement[2]	130.0	84.0	404.0	

Sources: 1. B. Barbieri, *I consumi nel primo secolo dell'unità d'Italia*, Milan: Giuffré, 1961, p. 46; 2. This was the 'normal' requirement for an adult male worker according to the 'Inchiesta sulle condizioni igeniche e sanitarie dei comuni del Regno' (Direzione Generale di Statistica, Rome, 1886) quoted in S. Somogyi, 'L'alimentazione nell'Italia unita', in *Storia d'Italia*, Vol. V, Book I, Turin: Einaudi, 1973, p. 850.

Note: Proteins, fats and carbohydrates are expressed in grammes. Calories: total number per day.

number of calories per head would be barely enough to nourish a manual worker,[15] there is no doubt that the highly unequal distribution of food resulted in widespread malnutrition. For example: at the end of the century the average per capita availability of meat was 16.7 kilogrammes a year for the country as a whole, but in the main urban centres this varied from a minimum of 31.5 kilogrammes in Sicily to a maximum of 89.8 kilogrammes in Sardinia. Urban consumption of meat was at least three times that of the average for the country as a whole: for the rural population (61 per cent of the labour force) meat seems to have been a luxury item consumed only a few times a year. In fact, out of fifteen peasant family budgets studied at the turn of the century, 'only in very few cases, clearly abnormal in composition, were there exceptions to the rule that the greater part of food came from cereals, legumes and fruit, which sometimes exceeded nine-tenths of expenditure.'[16] 'As the years went by', notes Somogyi, 'the living conditions of the lowest classes assumed less tragic characteristics, but Chessa, at the beginning of the century observed how the peasants in the province of Sassari ate almost only bread, which though of good quality was not enough to feed them adequately.'[17]

Another way to measure the overall improvement in the 'welfare' of a population relies on indicators such as infant mortality and average life expectancy in which the overall 'quality of life' plays a more important part than do advances in medicine.

At the beginning of the 1880s an Italian's life expectancy at birth was 35.4 years. Twenty years later this had risen to 42.8.[18] This improvement was due principally to the fall in infant mortality. At the time of the Unification 223 children per thousand live births died in their first year of life; by the eve of the First World War this figure had fallen to 138. Table 4.8 shows the comparative pattern of this variable, highlighting, on the one hand, the steady fall in the Italian infant mortality rate and, on the other, how levels in Italy compared favourably on an international level with countries where per capita income was higher.

Table 4.8 Mortality rates during the first year of life (per 1,000 live births)

Period	Italy	U.K.	France	Germany	Austria	Spain	Russia
1865−9	223	157	178	309	258	196	272
1880−4	201	142	170	231	251	192	275
1900−4	169	143	143	204	216	180	253
1910−14	138	108	118	163	187	151	254

Source: B.R. Mitchell, *European Historical Statistics 1750−1970*, London: Macmillan, 1975.

The improvement in 'welfare' can also be seen in the fall in aggregate mortality rates (Table 4.2: p. 27) which is reflected in another important indicator: the median age of death for males over the age of five − 49.2 and 63.5 years for 1865 and 1915 respectively.[19]

More complex is the evaluation of another overall index of a population's standard of living: the height of adult males, which depends not only on the quantity of food eaten during the first years of life, but also on its quality and on the environmental and hygiene conditions on which its assimilation depends. Studies on this matter are still only at the preliminary stage in Italy and many years will pass before they produce reliable results. Meanwhile, one may observe that average male height as measured during the medical examination for military service rose throughout the period dealt with in this volume, with the exception of the years 1868−71, rising from 161.92 centimetres (average for 1861−70) to 166.62 centimetres (average for 1911−20).

On the whole, indicators such as infant mortality, life expectancy, and height seemed to show a less discontinuous pattern than that of per capita income. While this, as already mentioned, did not rise until the end of the century, the improvement in the standard of living implicit in the behaviour of the above-mentioned indicators seems to have begun in the 1860s and 1870s and to have continued without a break until the Great War. The possible hypotheses are two: either the national accounting statistics are incorrect and do not measure the actual patterns in income and consumption, or these variables have no immediate effect on life expectancy and other similar indicators. Until the Italian national accounting series are revised and until non-descriptive studies on the problem of standards of living appear, it is impossible to say which of these hypotheses is the more plausible.

Chapter five

Before the Unification

The new demographic trend

'Between 1740 and 1750, in a stormy climate of uncertainty, the Italian economy [reached] both one of its most critical points and, at the same time, the limit beyond which lay the inversion of tendency.'[1] This was probably the period which saw the breaking of the 'Malthusian trap' which, in the sixteenth and seventeenth centuries, had caused the Italian population to oscillate between 10 and 12 million. According to Cipolla[2] this figure was to reach 17 million in 1770. More conservative estimates for the same year put the population of Italy at around 15 million.[3] In 1800 the population would reach 17.2 million, at the end of the Napoleonic wars 18.4 million and on the eve of the 1848 revolutions it would be 23.6 million, showing therefore a considerable acceleration of the trend[4] which had started[5] from a typically Malthusian increase aimed at filling the vacuum created by the last Great Plague of the seventeenth century. Around the middle of the following century this acceleration assumed features setting in motion 'the mechanism which allowed a marked excess of births over deaths.'[6]

These were probably the distant origins of modern economic growth in Italy – origins without either dramatic discontinuities or sudden spurts. The process was very slow and in its course the gap between Italy's national income and that in north-western Europe tended to widen.

The middle of the eighteenth century saw the beginning of an urban growth which was to continue for more than two centuries.[7] Given this and the fact that in 1861 58 per cent of the working population was employed in agriculture, one must conclude that, in the years around 1740, at least 60 to 65 per cent of Italians got their sustenance from the land.

The backwardness of Italy relative to Great Britain, *before* the latter began her own 'industrial revolution', becomes evident when considering that around the middle of the eighteenth century no more than 40 per cent of the total British working population was engaged in agriculture.[8] As far as the ratio of population to resources is concerned, it should be recalled that during the same period the population of Great Britain was around half that of the Italian peninsula which had an agrarian area only 30 to 35 per cent greater than that of the British Isles (excluding Ireland).

There are no estimates, however approximate, of the production trend between the mid-eighteenth and mid-nineteenth centuries, but the little information that does exist makes the hypothesis of a zero or very slow growth in per capita income highly plausible. Paul Bairoch's admittedly rough estimates of this variable for the years 1830 and 1850 imply an average annual growth of 0.2 per cent.[9] For the eighteenth century, the very fact that the increase in population was rather slow would make one favour, along with other considerations,[10] the hypothesis of an almost stationary per capita income level. The downward trend in mortality rates which began towards the mid-eighteenth century in due course led the demographic increase to settle at values which characterized modern economic growth in Italy, without a substantial increase in per capita income. This situation has a parallel, in very different historical circumstances, in numerous low-income countries in Asia, Africa, and Latin America during the present century.

The question of property rights

Some economic historians hold, in common with Marx, that an 'agricultural revolution' of some kind is a prerequisite, though not sufficient in itself, for getting modern economic growth under way. In particular, it is held that the feudal systems typical of 'traditional societies' hinder the increase of productivity in agriculture and the mobilization of production factors in that they hamper the free availability of the land on the part of those who possess it and the free availability of their work force on the part of the peasants.

Feudal institutions varied from region to region and adapted themselves during the course of the centuries to the productive and demographic characteristics of the individual areas in which they developed. Thus, in western Europe – roughly that part to the west of the Elbe and the Danube – serfdom rapidly disappeared from the twelfth century onwards. The Italian peninsula followed the western pattern: when the eighteenth century reformers posed the question of the abolition of fedualism, serfdom was a thing of the past.

The aristocracy's feudal privileges existing in the eighteenth century consisted in 'rights' to a variety of forms of tax collection and in a series of administrative, jurisdictional, and political powers. If in northern Italy the latter were already partially eroded,[11] in the south 'during the first decades of the eighteenth century the political, jurisdictional and economic power of the barony [were] still virtually intact.'[12] There, the process of overthrowing feudalism was particularly slow: at the end of the century the power of the barons was still extremely strong.

The anti-feudal polemic, already present in the work of Genovesi, was to assume in the 1780s 'the nature of a real offensive', of which Gaetano Filangeri was, in all probability, the initiator.[13] The objectives of the reformers were political and administrative as well as economic. In essence, the reformers advocated the creation of a modern state with an administrative system based on precise laws, run by a professional bureaucracy and with an impartial judicial system in which every citizen could both be and feel himself to be equal. The path towards the abolition of the remaining feudal privileges varied considerably from region to region. In Tuscany, from 1749 on, Grand Duke Francesco had kept for himself feudal privileges such as the administration of criminal justice, the rights to tribute in kind, and the selection and command of the troops. In 1771, in the Duchy of Modena the final vestiges of personal serfdom were done away with. While Lombardy enjoyed the reforms of Joseph II, the territory of the Serenissima Republic of Venice enjoyed a feudal code of 1780. Every feudal authority and right was finally abolished by the Cisalpine Republic in 1796.

The Neapolitan revolution of 1799, whose reforming legislation matured late and remained ineffectual, 'made the land-holding and agrarian bourgeoisie conscious of its class position between barons and peasants.'[14] This consciousness matured in the decade of French rule and was reflected in an extolling of private property, the very principle of which contrasted with many of the institutions, privileges, and jurisdictional forms of feudal origins. In other words, the idea was to make land freely available through the abolition of the so-called 'deeds of trust' which established the inalienability of feudal domains, and the tax on church lands. With the arrival of Joseph Bonaparte the *Code Napoleon* was extended to the Kingdom of the Two Sicilies. Since 1806, provision had been made for the sale of lands belonging to the state and their allotment to those who possessed them.[15] In the following two years, the state abolished religious and monastic orders, appropriated their lands and resold them, freeing them from any bond.

It should be noted that the abolition of feudalism in the south did not represent an 'agrarian reform' in the classic sense of a substantial change in land ownership. It was, in essence, an adjustment and better definition of property rights, but the land remained in the hands of the aristocracy. The actual redistribution of land was very limited and did not bring about a breaking up of the large landed estates, nor their subdivision into optimum size farms and their allocation to the farmer/capitalist: 65 per cent of the state assets sold in order to finance the war during the reigns of Joseph Bonaparte and Murat went to the advantage of a mere 154 people, including some of the major members of the Neapolitan nobility.[16] The bourgeoisie acquired above all medium size lots, but this did not lead them to become agrarian entrepreneurs.

An overall evaluation of the economic significance of the 'abolition' of feudalism – extended to Sicily during the reign of Ferdinand I – is anything but easy. It did not seem to create a large agricultural surplus and, in any case, only a small part of what was produced between 1815 and 1850 went to industrial investment. The social prestige and economic power of the landed artistocracy, although deprived of its administrative and jurisdictional functions, were barely touched. For at least another century the south, and the country as a whole, would bear the weight of the preservation of these powers. In Sardinia, feudal systems survived in part throughout the reign of Carlo Felice and were definitively suppressed, after 1832, by Carlo Alberto. The last laws regarding this matter were signed by Siccardi.[17]

Agriculture during the 1850s

At the end of 1849 'the political and electoral defeat of radical democracy was, in a certain sense, the premise for the realization of moderate and liberal progress, to be carried out through parliament, that the best men on the liberal side and, above all, Cavour hoped for.'[18]

Around the middle of the century, Italy, considering the present boundaries, had a population of about 24 million; about 36 per cent in the Kingdom of the Two Sicilies, and 40 per cent distributed equally between the Kingdoms of Sardinia and the Austrian Lombardo–Veneto (see Table 5.1).

Existing studies of Italy's economy before Unification,[19] given the poverty of quantitative source material, do not allow even the approximate formulation of convincing estimates as to the trend of Italian agricultural and industrial production during the decade preceding Unification. In these circumstances, Bairoch's estimates,[20] which would imply an average annual growth rate of 0.8 per cent in

Table 5.1 Population of the various Italian states around 1850 (in millions)

Kingdom of Sardinia	5.0
of which: Sardinia 0.55	
Savoy 0.58	
Lombardo–Veneto Kingdom	5.0
Grand Duchy of Tuscany	1.8
Papal States	3.0
Kingdom of the Two Sicilies	8.7
of which: Mainland 6.6	
Sicily 2.1	
Total	23.5
Italy's population within today's borders	24.0

Sources: For Piedmont: R. Romeo, *Cavour e il suo tempo*, Bari: Laterza, 1977, p. 883. For the other Italian states: M. Romani, *Storia economica d'Italia nel secolo XIX*, Bologna: Il Mulino, 1982, pp. 374–5.

real income per capita between 1850 and 1860, cannot be considered more than guesswork. One must therefore resist the temptation to speculate on the significance of the growth, however modest, which took place during those years.

It should be remembered, however, that the 1850s saw important industrial developments in England as well as in mainland Europe, and that the agricultural sector, characterized by rising prices, did relatively well taking the European economy as a whole.

It is not easy to formulate a synthetic judgement about agricultural production in Italy. As far as wheat is concerned, it can be said that

some increases (in production per hectare), even considerable ones after 1840–48, were registered in some parts of Emilia but, in general, the levels of unit yield did not undergo any changes worthy of note . . . in both North and South the techniques for the sowing, cultivation, and harvesting of wheat were backward. The agricultural implements were imperfect and of little use to the crop, the types of wheat known were easily flattened; continuous rotation either did not exist or was biennial; fertilizers – only stable manure – were used in insufficient quantities, often at the wrong time and in the wrong way.[21]

As well as the low dynamism of grain cultivation, where there was little response to the stimulus deriving from the international increase in prices, there were unfavourable circumstances both in vine and silkworm cultivation which were affected by parasitic diseases. In the first case it was cryptogram or oidium which from 1851–2 spread throughout the Italian peninsula hitting Lombardy, the Veneto, and Tuscany with particular virulence. In some cases, 'by 1852 the overall production of wine was reduced to a third of the 1838 level and in 1854 it fell to a little more than a tenth of the average for the period 1842–51.'[22] In the case of silkworms, pebrine 'already widespread from Piedmont to Friuli between 1854 and 1855 arrived in the Naples region the following year, spread everywhere from 1857 on . . . and seemed, by the end of the decade, to have more or less halved the overall average annual harvest.'[23]

Although the crisis hit hardest in the north, it was the south that suffered more in the long term. While in the north agriculture was sustained by irrigation and by livestock breeding, the south's hopes for diversifying and widening the range of products destined for national and international markets lay in wine and silk. In his study of the origins of Italy's economic dualism Luciano Cafagna highlights how, during the 1850s, the hopes southern producers had of becoming the main suppliers of cocoons for the numerous silk mills operating in northern Italy came to nothing.[24]

When cryptogram and pebrine spread in the southern provinces and when it became noticeable how quickly the local fruit and vegetable markets were saturated, it was apparent that the few improvements that had been introduced – vines, fruit, silk-worms – with the sole exception of oil, had had no great effect in diversifying a grain growing agrarian regime.[25]

In the south, therefore, the pre-Unification decade saw 'the progressive wearing out of the efforts that until 1848 had characterized the actions of the Bourbon governments, and was marked by a profound crisis at all levels.'[26] For Italy as a whole, there is considerable agreement among various scholars that while the 1850s saw no generalized progress in agriculture, there were serious crises in at least two important sectors. It is difficult, therefore, to see in the agricultural developments of the pre-Unification decade either that releasing of productive forces or that formation of surplus in rural areas, which the classical vision felt should have derived from anti-feudal agrarian reform seen as a prerequisite of modern economic growth.

Progress in industry

The 700–800 silk mills existing in Piedmont and Lombardy in the mid-nineteenth century employed about 150,000 workers, taking advantage of agricultural part-time work. 'It would be no exaggeration to assert that these small factories offered the first opportunity for industrial training to workers who were subsequently employed in other manufacturing industries.'[27] In this sense, the importance of silk yarn went beyond its ability to guarantee about one third of Italian exports.[28] Tied to the agriculture of the less fertile hill zones, this sector was somewhere between the so-called proto-industry and the modern factory system, and increased the purchasing power of farmers and peasant alike. It created a market for other manufactures, accounted for the spread of credit in rural areas, and gradually led to the creation of a small-businessman class as well as a new working class.

The cotton industry doubled the number of spindles in what is now called the 'industrial triangle' (Piedmont, Lombardy, Liguria). In this case too, it was a typically dualistic development in which types of cottage industry and modern factories (although often small) grew side by side. The wool industry already had some large factories in Piedmont, Lombardy, and the Veneto. The foothill areas in which it was possible to exploit both water power and the abundance of labour were those of higher settlement intensity of the small and medium-sized silk, wool, and cotton industries. The conditions of the Neapolitan cotton mills were different: concentrated for the most part around Salerno, they were originated by the state and managed by foreign entrepreneurs who often employed foreign (mainly Swiss) labour, and depended on government demand and high protectionist duties.[29]

Taking the future kingdom as a whole, the dimensions of those manufacturing industries which would constitute, from the end of the century onwards, the most dynamic sectors of modern economic growth in Italy, i.e. the metal-making, engineering, and chemical industries, were very modest. The data for these industries appear even more uncertain than those relating to the textile sector. For pig iron, an important indicator of economic development, the estimate by Romeo[30] of 29,000 tonnes produced at the end of the decade appears too low in the light of the fact that the Grand Duchy of Tuscany alone exported 31,000 tonnes in 1859.[31] Caracciolo's estimate of 60,000 tonnes is more credible.[32] In any case this was still very low when compared with production in the principal European countries.[33] The engineering industry was, for the most part, made up of small firms with few employees, more like a traditional workshop than a modern factory. There were exceptions, such as shipbuilding, in which the factory system and vertical integration with the steel industry were indispensable. Firms such as Giovanni Ansaldo and Giovanni Orlando were established before the Unification, and were destined to play an important role in Italy's industrial history, but the size and organization of these firms in this period were such that they could not compete with the leading foreign businesses.[34] In the Kingdom of Naples some shipbuilding and heavy engineering industries developed with the vital help of the state. The chemical industry was backward in comparison to that of western European countries: many firms were owned by foreigners and the main products were soap and perfume essences. Dyes, paint, and fertilizers were, for the most part, imported.

A certain prestige was maintained by some industries where a particularly qualified labour input was the best legacy of the organization and urban regulation of arts and crafts. The best examples were Venetian glass and crystal; Milanese, Tuscan, and Neapolitan ceramics and printing. Here too, for the most part, the statistics are incomplete, thus making it impossible to give an overall idea of the trend in industrial production during the 1850s.

Rail transport – the great innovation of the first half of the nineteenth century – made its appearance in the mid-1830s, at more or less the same time as in the rest of Europe, but its subsequent growth was far slower. In 1850 there were only 620 kilometres of track in the Italian peninsula. Its subsequent progress, however, was anything but insignificant: by 1860 the rail network of the new Kingdom totalled about 2,400 kilometres. Contrary to what happened in Germany during the same period, railway construction did not generate a substantial increase in domestic demand for iron, steel, and rolling stock. However, it may be assumed, by analogy with what happened in the following decades, and given the high labour intensity of railway construction, that there was an increase in the demand for wage-goods such as food and textiles.

Pre-Unification economic policies

Beginning with the enlightened reformism of the eighteenth century two apparently contrasting tendencies in economic policy, though with different forms and intensity, were taking shape. On one side the ideas of *laissez-faire* were gradually assuming practical importance in connection to the wider movement advocating greater political and personal freedom. On the other, the state, while divesting itself slowly of mercantilist trappings, took on new initiatives reforming the administration and the fiscal system, and, above all, increasing both fiscal pressure and expenditure, in particular for public works. In other words, side by side with the spread of free-trade ideology new and diverse initiatives were undertaken by the state. It has been noted that the two tendencies only seemed to be in contrast with one another: 'the very fact of wanting to apply *laissez-faire* in a situation still riddled with feudal bonds led to a favouring of economic liberty through state intervention.'[35] In the conditions of economic backwardness in mid-nineteenth century Italy the bourgeois stratum remained thin and did not find spontaneous assent for its own projects and interests: what the new class lacked was the autonomous political strength to induce a spontaneous reversal of absolutist mercantilism. The political power acquired by the moderate bourgeoisie, after the failure of the 1848 revolutions, allowed it to promote 'reforms from above' which gave the state new economic and bureaucratic strength.

Economists and reformers of European standard were present in eighteenth century Italy and at the moment of political unification. Ideas circulated in an elite which, though restricted, was destined to take the reins of the unified state. The Italian economists of the time were not mere propagators of the new English *laissez-faire*: a long tradition of intellectual links with France and Germany prevented them from falling into a new cultural provincialism. Italy's economic culture was pervaded by a certain eclecticism and there were those who talked of an 'Italian School', characterized by a strong and specific interest in empirical research, data gathering, and in a concrete, pragmatic analysis of reality.[36]

In this context and with this type of cultural support, new lines of economic policy could slowly affirm themselves almost everywhere. State intervention was identified less and less with protectionist practices and the minute codification of rules to be obeyed by producers. It assumed, slowly and not without contradictions, the form of more efficient bureaucratic structures; intervention for the abolition of centuries-old privileges; unification and streamlining of tariff systems; promotion of industries and new instruments of financial intermediation. Public expenditure, directed especially towards the creation of social overhead capital, grew more rapidly than national income.

In the context of these general tendencies, the economic policies pursued by the various governments differed greatly from state to state. In the Kingdom of the Two Sicilies, a more backward area but one with a lively economic culture, an interesting attempt at industrialization, promoted by the state and characterized by the considerable contribution of foreign capital, foreign technicians, and even foreign workers, had already been made at the end of the 1820s.[37] One of the pillars of Neapolitan economic policy was still the Customs. In 1823–4 there had been a tariff reform which made it more suited to serve the needs of industry. With a few exceptions, the important duties on raw materials had been abolished, while manufacturers had been granted considerable protection.[38] Moreover, the government had increased its own demand for national products, particularly army and navy supplies, and had given direct incentives to the metal-making and engineering manufacturing industries. Experimental firms had been created and run by the state: two such examples were the iron works at Mongiana and the engineering industry of Pietrarsa, created by Ferdinand II for the production of steam boilers for ships and railways, rolling stock, iron bridges, and the like. In the 1830s and 1840s manufacturing production in the Naples area had made considerable progress, especially in the textile (cotton, wool, and silk) and engineering sectors. On the whole, howver, direct and indirect state intervention had not succeeded in creating an adequate manufacturing industry, in part because this intervention was probably too limited and in part because the backward agricultural system was unable to generate significant demand for industrial products.

With the passing of time, free-trade ideas took hold throughout Italy. Between 1845 and 1846 Naples revised its import duties downwards.[39] In early 1847 Richard Cobden was enthusiastically received by both businessmen and government politicians from Turin to Naples. At the end of the same year, after the signing of trade and navigation treaties between Piedmont, Tuscany, and the Papal States, a declaration of principle was reached in favour of an Italian customs union. As with the *Zollverein*, the German customs union, political and economic motives were closely intertwined. The fact that the union never came about was certainly not without its consequences: as will be seen in the next chapter, the hasty way in which the customs unification of the country was to come about a decade later gave rise to not totally unjustified furious polemics.

The programmes and 'reforms' (some of which were destined to last) of the provisional revolutionary governments around 1848 were not generally of an exceptionally radical nature.[40] Rather, they constituted the acceleration and, in some cases, the maturation of ideas and administrative measures inspired by the new principle of liberty; of uniformity and precision of the law; of objective and efficient administration which had gradually absorbed something of the spirit of the age. The importance of this acceleration and maturation for the adoption of new economic policies must not be underestimated. In Piedmont, in 1851, a decidedly free-trade tariff was introduced, which was both preceded and followed by important trade treaties. The already modest duties of the Grand Duchy of Tuscany were reduced still further with a series of decrees in the period 1851−4.[41] Austria abandoned the almost prohibitionist system which had until then characterized her customs policy and reformed her own external tariffs in 1853−4, and, most important of all, abolished numerous internal duties within the Empire.[42] In Rome, in 1851, an enquiry conducted by the Chamber of Commerce revealed the widespread desire among businessmen for a reduction in import duties. This came about in June 1855.[43]

The economic policy in the Kingdom of Sardinia after the promulgation of the Albertine Constitution is particularly interesting given the role that Piedmontese politicians and ideas were to have during the first phase of the unification of Italy's economy. It has been noted on this point that

the maturation of the social body, the modernization of economic structures, the consolidation of a certain institutional framework, and the affirmation of a new ruling class, appeared to have proceeded with such consistency, like a kind of unitary historical block, that it is difficult to consider them separately.[44]

Nor should we forget the close interdependence between economic policy and politics *tout court* that prevailed during the 1850s. Economic policy was literally dominated by the Piedmontese plan to substitute Austria in her hegemonic position in Italian affairs.

When he became Minister of Agriculture and Trade in 1850, Cavour immediately signed trade treaties with Belgium and England thus opening the way for the Tariff Act of July 1851, which marked a radical change of policy towards free trade. Specific duties were replaced with *ad valorem* duties: they were limited to 1−5 per cent for raw materials destined for agriculture, and fixed at around 10 per cent for the majority of consumer goods, except for luxuries. Imports of some raw materials (wool, cotton, coal, iron ore) were free of duty. The 1851 Tariff Act marked an important change in economic policy, with some improvements it provided the basis for the first Italian Tariff whose free trade inspiration was to last until 1878.

Piedmontese fiscal policy aimed, in the 1850s, at the reduction of the considerable budget deficit created by expenditure on the 1849 war, by interest payments on the large debts contracted on that occasion and by the indemnity to Austria. Between 1849 and 1858 this deficit was reduced from 108 million to 17 million lire.[45] This was achieved almost exclusively by an increase of tax revenue which rose, between 1850 and 1858, by 5.2 per cent a year while expenditure fluctuated around an essentially stable level. Indirect taxation in 1858 accounted for more than 56 per cent of income, even if its weight had been falling gradually due to the introduction, albeit rather low-key, of direct taxes. On the expenditure side, there was an increase in the weight of defence due to the political reasons outlined above. For Cavour the creation of an efficient infrastructure was perhaps the most important contribution that the state could make towards the growth of private industry. For this purpose, despite great budgetary difficulties, he involved the government in an important railway programme. In part this was carried out directly by the state, in part with the promotion of 'very wide contracts'[46] with private enterprises. In 1858 Piedmont had a rail network of 830 kilometres. To the railways were added roads, telegraph, and port facilities.

In 1849, manoeuvring behind the scenes, Cavour succeeded in bringing about the merger of the two banks of issue into one Banca Nazionale degli Stati Sardi which was subsequently to obtain government help in maintaining the monopoly of issue, increasing capital, and opening branches in all the provinces. This move met with violent opposition from those who did not believe liberal principles and monopoly of issue to be compatible. Compromise was reached with the return to the gold standard, which, however, 'ultimately slowed down the affirmation of bank note circulation in the Sardinian states, making the Bank's contribution to the country's economic development less extended and less effective.'[47] For the rest, Piedmontese financial intermediation in these years remained prevalently in the hands of the private banking houses of Genoa and Turin. The Cassa Depositi e Prestiti was reorganized; steps were taken to regulate and promote the birth of Savings banks, and the administration of the Opere Pie di San Paolo — destined to become an important bank — was handed over to lay authorities.[48]

Chapter six

Economic problems of the Unification

Economics and politics in the Unification process

'The protagonists of the Risorgimento – with a few exceptions (the most important of whom was Cavour) – were not, on the whole, very sensitive to that irreplaceable, dynamic and unifactory element which is economic growth.'[1] In this sense the contrast with Germany – the other great European country during this period to undergo a process of national unification – is marked. The customs union (*Zollverein*) in Germany, realized between 1817 and 1834, was part of a design, certainly not without its contrasts and contradictions, in which market integration was seen as an indispensable prerequisite of national unification. In the 1850s and 1860s the railways, big business, and the banks operated in Germany as factors both of development and national economic unification so that, even taking the dualistic nature of Germany's economy into consideration, it can be said that by the time the Reich was proclaimed, Germany had already taken the most crucial steps towards the creation of a single national market and was on the path towards modern economic growth.

In Italy the customs union had remained at the project stage; the railway network had progressed far more slowly and in a less organic way than elsewhere; and, with the exception of Piedmont and Tuscany, economic reforms had been rather timid. On the whole, the participation of manufacturing interests in the Risorgimento was virtually non-existent and the leadership of the movement was assumed by the moderate representatives of Piedmontese and Tuscan agrarian interests and by a great number of the exponents of the professional middle class. The representatives of the popular masses were completely excluded from this political process.

As viewed by Carocci,

The fundamental factors in the Unification of Italy were culture and diplomacy. It was what nowadays would be termed a 'reform from above', which, despite its democratic basis, aimed more at containing the two factors – revolutionary and military – capable of mobilizing the masses.[2]

The process of political unification was accomplished with a rapidity which surprised even the protagonists themselves and which resulted in precarious political and social equilibria both at home and abroad. The moderate Right, with the backing of a very small number of citizens, miraculously succeeded in bringing about the political unification of the country, operating in the restricted area of common ground between divergent interests and often presenting itself as the lesser evil for each of the forces in the field. By operating in this way, Cavour and his followers guaranteed the birth and survival of the new state. This was made possible by the abandonment of their original consistent liberal design; by the constant search for compromises with the representatives of the most important vested interests they aimed at keeping an acceptable degree of consensus at home, containing democratic pressure, and avoiding armed intervention by France and Austria.

In this way the new state succeeded in overcoming the difficult early years of its existence despite the military defeat of 1866, Garibaldi's exploits, the indifference of the masses in the centre–north and the widespread discontent in the south, which made it necessary to station 200,000 soldiers there. In such circumstances as these the solutions to many problems and the formulation of consistent and far-reaching economic policies had to be sacrificed to the common good. The indispensable search for the widest possible consensus would be carried out in successive political equilibria from the alliances made by Cavour to the transformism of Depretis and right up to the different forms of Giolittism. On the economico-social ground this search would imply unnatural alliances between the tenant farmers of the Po valley and the absentee landlords of the south, and between the latter and the developing manufacturing industries.

The structural problems: backwardness and dualism

It has been noted that after the Unification, Italy was the 'sixth great power of Europe', and was recognized as such at the Congress of London in 1863.[3] The factor which transformed Italy – Metternich's 'mere geographical expression' – into a continental power was demographic size rather than political status or economic prosperity.[4] It was a giant with feet of clay.

Politically, Italy was 'a satellite state, a vassal state of Imperial

France: a state with insufficient internal capacities, with her finances in ruins, tormented between reaction and revolution, with the Pope excommunicating from Rome, and Garibaldi and Mazzini always in search of revolutionary adventures.'[5] However, it was especially from the economic point of view that the 'sixth power' showed all its weakness. Despite the extreme uncertainty of per capita income estimates relative to this period and the complexity of international comparisons on this subject, the sheer size of the gap between Italy and the more advanced Western countries was such as to leave little doubt as to its relative position. The United Kingdom, the Low Countries, Switzerland, Belgium, and France itself probably reached per capita income levels, in 1861, somewhere between twice and one-and-a-half times those in Italy.[6] Raw cotton consumption did not reach 3 per cent of that in Britain, 9 per cent of that in France, nor 11 per cent that of Germany.[7] As to so-called heavy industry, one need only mention that production of pig iron at the beginning of the 1870s equalled only a fifth of that in a small and backward country such as Hungary.[8] The railways, an over-valued but not negligible symbol of progress in the years around Unification, had about 2,400 kilometres of track through-out the peninsula (1860) – equal to that of Spain and not very much more than in tiny Belgium.[9]

This overall backwardness was coupled with an exceptional variety of local situations: it is not by chance that reference is made not to one but to several 'economic Italies'.[10] There is no doubt that striking regional differences and, particularly, the considerable gap between the level of economic development in the north-western area and that in the southern part of the country constituted an important peculiarity of the 'Italian case' in the context of European modern economic growth during the last century. The scanty statistical evidence available leaves no doubt as to the dimensions of this dualism. Luzzatto underlines the demographic slump of the urban centres, excepting Milan, Genoa, Turin, and Florence.[11] The illiteracy rate was around 50 to 55 per cent in Piedmont and Lombardy, but as high as 86 to 90 per cent in the various provinces of the Kingdom of the Two Sicilies. The latter had only 5 per cent of the Italian capital invested in joint-stock companies[12] and a similar percentage of kilometres of working railway line. As to agriculture, while it was true that in both north and south there was 'land whose yield exceeded 15 quintals per hectare',[13] it was also true that the most striking and serious indicator of the gap between north and south at the Unification was the enormous seasonal unemployment of peasants in the south 'given that wheat required only thirty working days a year and the vine only twice or three times as much.'[14]

Low levels of accumulation and income per capita, plus an exceptionally pronounced interregional gap were, therefore, the two great and closely intertwined structural problems of the Kingdom of Italy proclaimed in March 1861. In spite of Italy's remarkable industrialization during the twentieth century, dualism remains even now its greatest unresolved problem.

The organization of the state

Although the question of the state institutions which were taking shape during the years of the Unification had far wider and more complex implications than those relative to modern economic growth, the dynamics of the latter was closely linked to that of the state's political and administrative organization. The legislation passed in the first years after the Unification was often to last for a good many years.

The moderate elite which led the country during the final phases of the Risorgimento and the early days of unified Italy had no doubts as to the setting up of the new state as a monarchy under the Albertine Constitution of the Kingdom of Sardinia. There was also basic agreement on the point that the active electorate should be confined to a limited number of male citizens: that is, those who paid direct taxes for sums which varied according to the region and the particular business activity undertaken. At the first elections (in late January/early February 1861) 418,696 citizens had the right to vote out of a population of almost 22 million.[15] The maintenance of such a restricted electoral suffrage law accentuated the oligarchic nature of the institutions in the new Kingdom and made the participation of the masses in the life of the state virtually impossible. Such participation would come about only 'through violent crises' which would contribute to the fragility of the social fabric, and would have negative implications for economic growth itself.[16]

Both in the Piedmontese parliament and within the moderate group itself, led by Cavour, there were anything but marginal differences of opinion as to the problems of local self-government. The idea of following the English pattern, characterized by a strong decentralization of administrative powers, seemed at a certain point to have the upper hand: it appealed to Cavour himself who, however, was not unaware of its inherent dangers. In the King's Speech in April 1860, Victor Emmanuel said on this point:

Founded on the Constitution, with political, military and financial unity and the uniformity of civil and penal laws, the progressive liberty of province and commune will renew in the

Italian peoples that splendid and vigorous life which in other forms of civilization and of European organization was the outcome of self-government.[17]

In essence, the government proposed first of all the creation of a centralized state, but did not exclude, and indeed hoped for, a progressive devolution of power to local authorities. In March 1861, Minghetti presented parliamentary bills for the devolution to municipalities, districts, and provinces of powers that the Piedmontese administrative Act of 1859 had reserved for central government. In presenting these bills, the Minister of the Interior began by saying: 'our aim is to grant the various parts of the Kingdom the maximum possible number of administrative privileges, providing that national unity remain whole and, indeed, that it be further consolidated.'[18]

However, these bills met with strong opposition and were withdrawn after Cavour's death. In October 1861, Ricasoli extended Piedmontese law to the whole Kingdom. The debate dragged on until the passing in March 1865 of a new municipal and provincial law which, however, 'differed only slightly from that of October 1859.'[19]

The reasons for the prevalence of the more extreme tendencies in favour of a bureaucratic and administrative organization along Napoleonic lines were many. They could be found, first of all, in the insecurity of the moderate ruling class who thought it safer to leave the least possible space open for reactionary revivals and outbreaks of social revolt.[20]

However, the easy triumph of the centralization tendencies over the vision of devolution along Anglo-Saxon lines depended to a considerable extent on the country's backward conditions.[21] A vicious circle linked low levels of consumption and accumulation and the low expectations of growth to widespread values and traditions typical of a backward agrarian society, to the existence of a suffocated and short-sighted bourgeoisie and to the habit — particularly deep-rooted in the south — of relying as much on the paternalism of the state as, on a local level, on clientele systems and personal patronage. It was the annexation of the southern provinces that led Cavour and his central and northern followers to a rethinking of the previous liberal approaches to schemes of self-government when they found themselves 'faced with a social and political reality which those schemes had failed to foresee.'[22] On the other hand, the majority of liberals in the south was not in agreement with Crispi's opinion (later to change radically) that 'administrative centralization [was] a great evil and its development [threatened] liberties in Italy's present conditions.'[23] The parliamentary debate of April 1861 highlighted the narrow views and the fears of the majority of southern members whose requests boiled down to a limited programme of public works for relief purposes and to a reorganization and strengthening of the security forces.[24] The southern bourgeoisie was probably not wrong in fearing that it would be brushed aside by the old, though not any the less weak, aristocracy or by popular revolts were there to be no provision made for the stationing of Royal Carabinieri in every village.

There were, in theory, good reasons for preferring a centralist solution in a backward country such as Italy was in the last century if there exist both the political will and the capacity to break with the traditions and blocks of power which had resulted in poverty and dualism. However, as we have seen, the reasons for choosing a centralized institutional organization along French lines were not based on great designs for development, but rather on the need to survive of the moderate ruling class. The inadequacy of the Piedmontese regulations in serving as central instruments for the promotion of development, and the unpreparedness of the administrative bureaucratic apparatus to perform such an important task would contribute to a further fossilization of the system.

Free trade

Contrary to what happened in other sectors of social, administrative, and economic life, Italy's customs unification was brought about in the most sudden and radical of ways. The Piedmontese Tariff of 1859 was extended, with hardly any modifications, to the territories which were gradually uniting themselves to form the Kingdom of Italy. The trade and navigation treaties of the old states were replaced by those already in force in the Kingdom of Sardinia, which were based on free trade philosophy. Moreover, in the summer of 1860, the Finance Minister, Vegezzi, decreed a series of reductions in customs duties on textiles and woollen yarn, cotton, silk, linen, canvas, and other textile products which went from a half to a third of the duty.

The fact that such an important economic policy measure was brought to term without being undermined by the compromises typical of most of the choices made both then and in successive periods of post-Unification history depended on various circumstances. First of all, it was a measure reflecting the ideology of the moderate Piedmontese liberals, which summarized and symbolized the strategy of economic growth they advocated during the 1850s.

Before the appearance in parliament of old and new interests, the drive towards free trade met with agreement precisely because of its ideological references. The importance of Cavour's leadership should not be underestimated. The conversion into law of the Vegezzi bills gave the Prime Minister the opportunity to describe to parliament his own strategic vision of Italian economic growth. In Romeo's words, his speech was 'the swansong of the great fighter for free trade and the last time that he succeeded in gaining approval for a bill in favour of economic freedom.'[25]

One should not forget the other circumstances of a more general order which, however quick and clumsy, were the driving forces towards free trade. The entire cultural and political climate of western Europe had been oriented in that direction since the early 1850s and the movement culminated in 1860 with the signing of the Cobden–Chevalier commercial treaty between the United Kingdom and France, constructed on free trade bases which very soon, through the operating of the 'most favoured nation' clause, involved the *Zollverein*. The decade which began with the Unification of Italy was one, therefore, which saw customs duties at their lowest throughout the continent: in order to find analogous situation one would have to wait until the signing of the Treaty of Rome a century later. The cultural climate and a desire not to be excluded from the great European movement was a stimulus in the direction of free trade. This was not enough, however; an important driving force behind free trade came from 'new and pressing political reasons linked to the need of the new state to consolidate its formation through the maintenance of alliances and English and French sympathies.'[26] In June 1862 a treaty, characterized by its extreme free tradism, the terms of which Cavour had probably begun to negotiate in March of the previous year, was signed with France.

The extension to all the territories in the Kingdom of the 1859 Sardinian tariff may be criticized on technical grounds for the way in which it was carried out and, more generally, on its role in delaying development in the south. As to the first aspect, it is easy to observe that the measures for the creation of a customs union – from the *Zollverein* to those under the Habsburg monarchy, right up to the EEC – are normally carried out in a gradual way to allow time for the reallocation of production factors, which only in theory takes place instantaneously. The Italian case was an exception to this rule of common sense and good administration. The speed in which, with one stroke of the pen, the new tariff replaced the existing ones was not the best technical solution to the problem.

A comprehensive evaluation of the long-term effects of free trade is more complex and will be discussed later. For the moment, it is enough to say that the problem has been held relevant especially as regards the 'southern question'. Tuscany, in fact, already enjoyed a tariff regime similar to that in Piedmont; while Lombardy, with its highly productive agricultural system, was able to take advantage of free trade and its textile industry was strong enough to withstand its repercussions; finally, in the Papal territories, there was no industrial base worthy of the name to risk being damaged by the new tariff. Therefore, the problem concerned the southern provinces where, as we saw in the last chapter, manufacturing industries (mainly textile and engineering) of not inconsiderable size had developed behind the shield of tariffs. There were those who held that a less radical customs policy, sensitive to the needs of industry, would have preserved the industional base in the region around Naples. The advocates of free trade, on the other hand, maintained that businesses incapable of facing competition made an inefficient use of resources and that their loss was not to be regretted. This was, in essence, the age-old *querelle* between protectionists and free-traders, which, either rightly or wrongly, epitomized the resentment of many of the southern populations at least as regards the way in which the annexation of the Kingdom of the Two Sicilies had been carried out. It should be said, however, on the one hand that the dimensions of southern industry in the 1860s hardly justify the economies of scale argument for the protection of infant industry and, more importantly, on the other, that the south of Italy continued for several decades to enjoy 'non-tariff protection', due principally to high transport costs.

Unification of public finance

The differences in the economic policy pursued by the individual pre-Unification states, already mentioned in the previous chapter, were reflected in the diversity of the tax systems and the size of outstanding per capita debt in 1859. The extra revenues that had to be raised for war purposes made the situation the first national governments had to face even more difficult and intricate.

Bastogi, who had become Finance Minister in March 1861, took the first steps towards the creation of the Register of Public Debt in which were recorded all the debts of the pre-Unification state. They amounted to 3,103 million lire, and were converted for the most part into Italian 5 per cent Consols.[27] The new state began its existence with an outstanding debt equal to about 40 per cent of

GDP. However, the burden was not equally distributed among the citizens of the above-mentioned states. After subtracting the debt incurred during the War of Independence, per capita debt was 188 lire for the citizens of the ex-Kingdom of Sardinia; 84 lire for those in the ex-Kingdom of the Two Sicilies, and 55 lire for the Tuscans.[28] The deficit of the 1850s had served to provide Piedmont and other northern areas with social overhead capital; the unification of the debt implied a transfer of real resources from the south to the north of the country.

Budget deficits were very high in the first years, in part because of the slowness and inefficiency of the financial administration but, mainly, because of the political difficulty in dampening down the great hopes of Risorgimento for renewal with higher fiscal pressure. The issue of new Italian 5 per cent Consols was therefore inevitable. Its cost was particularly high since, given the uncertainties about the future of the new kingdom, they were quoted at 70.5 per cent of the par.

Tax unification was neither as simple nor as relatively painless as that of the public debt. The diversities in the fiscal regimes of the various pre-Unification states were many. To the need to reach a unified legislation affecting deeply-rooted traditions was added the even more unpopular need to procure new income for the Treasury. Bastogi proposed, and had approved by parliament, laws for the unification of stamp duty and death duties as well as those regarding Church lands and government concessions. The taxes on salt and tobacco, and the government monopoly on the latter, were extended throughout the new Kingdom. These measures met with a certain amount of protest, especially in the south where the Bourbons' traditional light-handedness in fiscal matters had corresponded to a relatively low level of public spending. However, the process of unifying and reording the taxation system had only just begun. In 1862 Sella, who had succeeded Bastogi at the Ministry of Finance, prepared a bill for the introduction of an income tax. In his opinion, income rather than capital was 'the only reason for which the individual citizen might feel bound to take in an annual expenditure made for the benefit of all.'[29] The importance of this tax, which Minghetti had passed by parliament in July 1863, lay more in the modernity of the principle which had inspired it than in the amount raised – the yield in the early years was only about 4 per cent of total revenue.

As will be seen in the next chapter, financial unification and reform proceeded slowly and rather untidily in that they were based more on growing expenditure requirements than on any precise, organic design.

Monetary unification

Money circulation in the pre-Unification states consisted mainly of metal coins, some of which were 'debased', that is their intrinsic value was inferior to face value. During the first half of 1861 attempts were made to withdraw these and replace them with newly-minted pieces. An Act in July of the same year established the exchange rate between the different coins in circulation and the Piedmontese lira. The limited number of notes in circulation, and of other means of bank payments, made the spread of the new monetary unit very slow. It is not difficult to imagine the psychological resistance to changes in the unit of account, and even in the design of the coins, in a population whose literacy was often low and whose attachment to local traditions was strong.

The most important formal measure for the unification of coinage circulation in the country was the Act of 24 August 1862, which created the Italian lira – equal in value to the Piedmontese lira – as unit of account and legal tender. The same law established the metal content of the lira on the basis of a measure introduced the previous December, which had fixed the ratio between the official prices of gold and silver at 15.59.[30] The reference model was that of the French *franc germinale* based on a bi-metallic standard of necessity destined to have a difficult life.[31] In fact, during these first years the system was based on a silver standard. In March 1863 the official exchange rate of the pound sterling was fixed at 25.3 lire and this was to remain unchanged, during the periods of convertibility, until July 1914.

An important problem, connected with monetary unification, was that of the banks of issue. It has been seen how Cavour had manoeuvred for the merger of the two Piedmontese banks of issue into the Banca Nazionale degli Stati Sardi. From that episode it may be argued that, in 1860–1, he was still (in principle at least) in favour of granting the monopoly of issue to one large bank. The line followed, however, was quite different. The Banca Nazionale degli Stati Sardi became the Banca Nazionale nel Regno[32] but succeeded only in absorbing two small banks of issue. Furthermore, while Cavour was still alive, the provisional Florentine government authorized, in 1860, the creation of a second Tuscan bank of issue (the Banca Toscana di Credito). There were thus five banks of issue operating in the new Kingdom at the time of political Unification. To these would be added, in 1870, the Banca Romana. The project for the unification of issuing rights was defeated by particularisms and local interests: the political equilibria of the time would probably have been unsettled by the granting of issuing monopoly to the ex-Banca Sarda. It should not be forgotten that in this period that banks of issue were undertaking short-and long-term credit. They were, in essence, the only large banks in the country. Issuing, on the other hand, formed a considerable part of their liabilities in an environment in which bank deposits were spreading very slowly. Given these circumstances, it is easy to understand the aversion felt in the financial circles of the ex-capitals for the concentration of such a large quota of the country's banking business in the hands of a single large national bank. A serious financial crisis, which was to involve all the banks of issue, was needed before the first big step could be taken (1893) towards monopoly which would ultimately be achieved only in 1926.

It should be noted that, in 1862, coin circulation was estimated at about 1,800 million lire as against the 200 million lire in banknotes. Only the progressive extension in the use of the latter led in successive years to the real monetary unification of the country. The decisive step for a widespread acceptance of the Italian lira as unit of account and banknotes as means of payment was taken with the suspension of metal convertibility of the lira discussed in the next chapter. Despite the maintenance of issuing plurality, the privileged link established between the government and the *Banca Nazionale*, made the latter the hinge of the country's monetary and banking system. During this period the banks of issue operated as normal credit institutions not scorning long-term operations and, as such, they constituted the embryonic structure of the financial intermediation system in the new Kingdom. However, 'medium- and long-term credit were still reserved, for the most part, for private bankers.'[33] The most important financial centres were Genoa, Livorno, Milan, and Turin. At the time of the Unification there were, moreover, a series of small local banks, in particular Savings Banks – the first of which had been founded in Venice in 1822 and the second in Milan a year later – and co-operative banks.

Political unification and the announcement of large-scale railway construction programmes promised high financial intermediation incomes. Between 1862 and 1865 twelve new deposit banks were created, some of which failed within a few years. Other institutions had more solid foundations and were to play an important role in successive decades. One among these merits particular attention: the Società Generale di Credito Mobiliare Italiano, founded in Turin in 1863 on the initiative of the French Crédit Mobilier of the Péreire brothers and of a group of local bankers. Managed by Domenico Balduino until 1885, the Credito Mobiliare, although committing itself heavily to the railway project, would avoid repeating the mistakes made by its French headquarters from which it was soon to free itself. Among the other banks founded in the early years after Unification, we should mention the Banca Anglo-Italiana, the Banca di Credito Italiano, the Banco di Sconto e Sete, and the Cassa Nazionale di Sconto Toscana. Although late in comparison to other European countries, these were the first steps towards the creation of a modern banking system capable of unifying the credit market: judging by the continuing differences in interest rates in various parts of the country for essentially similar operations, it must be concluded that several decades would have to pass before a full unification of money markets could take place.

Chapter seven

The 'Age of the Right'

Slow growth in a climate of uncertainty

According to the Fuà estimates, per capita income remained
virtually stationary during the years when the Right was in power.
At a macroeconomic level this is the main phenomenon of the
1860s and 1870s requiring both further investigation and explanation.

Romeo has solved the problem by denying its existence. 'This
was', he wrote, 'undoubtedly one of the periods of most rapid
progress that Italian agriculture has ever known.'[1] Given that the
primary sector was by far the most important and moreover, that
per capita industrial production increased by 1 per cent per
annum,[2] the overall evaluation of these years might actually be
overturned were this judgement based on solid statistical evidence.
But this is is not the way things stand. Romeo uses the ISTAT
series[3] which are only moderately more optimistic than those re-
examined by Orlando for the Fuà group: the former give an annual
per capita agricultural production growth rate of 0.5, the latter one
of 0.1.[4] Given the high margin of error implicit in this type of
reconstruction, the difference between the two figures cannot be
considered very significant.

Even in the light of the more optimistic estimates, the growth of
per capita income remained below that taken by Kuznets as the
threshold for modern economic growth. This may go some way to
explaining the disappointment that many, especially among the
bourgeoisie, felt after the hopes raised during the process of
political unification.

The international economic picture of the period saw a relatively
rapid development of the leading countries in Western Europe:
between 1861 and 1876 English domestic product grew by about 2.2
per cent per annum, that of Germany by 3.0 per cent. The French
economy had perhaps lost the shine of the 1850s but it continued to

grow. In America development got under way again from 1866–7 after the end of the Civil War. Free-tradism tended to dominate the international scene. However, the optimism of the 1850s was slowly fading above all because of the wars in Europe: between Austria and France in 1859; between Austria and Prussia in 1866, and, above all, the Franco-Prussian war of 1870 which led to the proclamation of the Reich in a defeated and humiliated Paris which would not easily forget the shame inflicted. The war reparation paid to Berlin was probably one of the causes of the speculation fever and of the successive financial crisis which exploded there in 1873 and then spread to other European stock markets. Although the real effects of this crisis were probably not very great, it symbolizeu the end of a period of growth which was replaced, from the mid-1870s on, by a real or presumed 'great depression' lasting twenty years.

The creation itself of a much larger Kingdom of Italy than either France or England would have wished disturbed the pre-existing equilibrium which, in the course of the following decade, was put much more radically to the test with the definitive emergence of the German Reich as the most important continental power. This context – which obliged the Italian governments to maintain an army out of proportion to the country's resources — must be kept in mind when studying the trend of economic variables during the 'Age of the Right'. One must also consider the internal situation of the country which was characterized by centuries-old divisions; the prevalence of local interests; extreme difficulties in communications (the linguistic unification of the Italian peninsula was not even on the horizon); and by the considerable lack of mass support – mainly, but not only, in the south – for the country's unification. The internal and international situation, the defeats of 1866, the restlessness of Garibaldi, and the tension of the months before September 1870 were certainly not such as to contribute to the climate of stable expectations which best favours the emergence of entrepreneurial animal spirits.

The problems of public finance

The Right led twelve governments between 1861 and 1876. The Ministry of Finance, the key ministry for the conduct of economic affairs, was held successively by such personalities as Bastogi, Sella, Minghetti, Scialoja, Ferrara, Rattazzi, Cambray-Digny. It was not easy, however, after the death of Cavour and faced with new and unexpected circumstances, to define a consistent 'line' of economic policy. A certain guiding principle may be found in the role – envisaged by Cavour – for the state in the promotion of growth: creation of more favourable conditions for private enterprise through the dismantling of the remaining mercantilist rules on the one hand, and the formation of social overhead capital (roads, ports, canals, and particularly railways) on the other. The latter, however, found its limits in the precepts of the financial orthodoxy of the time which postulated a balanced budget. The circumstances, however, were such that the Ministers of Finance were forced to make considerable compromises with their own principles.

In 1862 tax revenue covered only half of state expenditure, and the public debt accumulated up to that moment[5] was equal to 38 per cent of GDP. Piedmontese taxation was already giving rise to considerable discontent, especially in the south. On the other hand, it was impossible to reduce expenditure, given the rigidity of most items, particularly debt servicing and defence. Thence the further rapid expansion of debt. In 1866, when existing public debt had already reached 72 per cent of GDP, the war against Austria on the side of Prussia made further, urgent demands on the Treasury. The issue of new bonds could be done by discounting a high risk premium. The government decided, therefore, to turn to the Banca Nazionale del Regno for a loan of 250 million lire. The Bank asked, as counterpart, the authorization to suspend metal convertibility of its notes. The metal standard was suspended on 1 May 1866. The financial needs of the government were not limited to the first 250 million: the total amount of the loans at the end exceeded 600 million lire.[6] After the war, however, the budget deficit, which in 1866 reached 8 per cent of GDP, was slowly reduced by a careful expenditure policy and by a considerable increase in revenue. In 1876 the state budget was virtually balanced. The outstanding public debt, however, remained at a high level (92 per cent of GDP). Balancing the budget was without doubt one of the most important aspects of the economic policy of the time.

Sella's first attempts to increase revenue and reduce expenditure between 1864 and 1865 failed because of the war. When it ended Scialoja – Finance Minister during the difficult months of the suspension of the gold standard – tried to increase fiscal pressure by reforming existing direct taxation and, above all, by increasing indirect taxes such as the duty on wheat. His successors resorted to measures of extraordinary finance such as auctioning the Church lands previously nationalized by the state. This operation, however, yielded limited benefits to public finances. A tax of general character and easy collection was thought of: the grist tax. A tax on revenues from public debt yields, abolished some years earlier, was then reintroduced. In 1869 Sella returned to the Finance Ministry and remained there until 1873 taking a series of measures aimed mainly at improving efficiency in tax collection, which raised the state revenue from 850 to 1,010 million lire, and brought the deficit down to only 1 per cent of GDP.

The suspension of the gold standard

The suspension of the gold standard was seen as a national tragedy. Parliament set up a special Inquiry Committee. The debate was impassioned: one need only recall Ferrara's harsh words spoken in the Lower Chamber against the Minister Scialoja.[7] Even those who justified the government's operations did so emphasizing the dramatic situation which precluded any other solution.

A thorough study has yet to be made of the effects of the suspension of the gold standard on the most important economic variables. The hypotheses that we can advance on the likely direction of such effects seem, however, to lead to a rather positive evaluation of the measure taken in May 1866.

The suspension of the gold standard resulted in an increase in the price of gold in lire (in other words, a devaluation of the exchange rate of the lira).[8] This was about 8 per cent in 1866 and 7.4 per cent in the following year.[9] The increase in prices was not so marked: 4.5 and 0.5 respectively in 1866 and 1867.[10] Italian products, therefore, became more competitive on foreign markets with a resulting increase in exports. Moreover, since duties were collected in gold, the devaluation implied a proportional increase in import duties. On the whole, the suspension of the gold standard gave rise to greater demand for Italian products both abroad and on the home market. In fact, between 1865 and 1867 the Italian foreign trade deficit fell from 367 to 109 million lire. It is impossible to say how much of this improvement was due to the devaluation of the currency but in all likelihood its effects were not negligible. Furthermore the increase in domestic prices produced a reduction in the real value of the outstanding debt while part of the new issue, related to the war, could be monetized (the interest of 1.5 per cent which the state pledged to give the Banca Nazionale was lower than the rate of inflation).

The long-term effects of the suspension of the gold standard on the monetary system and on financial intermediation, although difficult to quantify, appear much more important. It must be said, first of all, that only with the measure of May 1866 was there an acceleration in the monetary unification of the country, which until then had proceeded very slowly. Coins were replaced by paper money which until then had been issued only in large denomination bills. The suspension of the gold standard brought the public nearer to banking intermediaries and favoured the growth of the latter. The banks of issue, which managed a sizeable quota of short- and long-term banking operations were able to increase their discounts and advances. The new commercial bank created along French lines – the Credito Mobiliare – found business easier in a world which until then had regarded paper money and banking deposits with suspicion. The effects of the suspension of the gold standard were obviously not limited to the years 1866–7. On the contrary, they proceeded slowly but then remained in the mentality and daily behaviour of a large mass of ordinary people. The suspension of the gold standard led to the spread, in time, of the first great 'modern' monetary innovations: paper money and bank deposits. This was a permanent contribution to economic growth in that it reduced transaction costs.

At the parliamentary Inquiry Committee it was affirmed that the Banca Nazionale had put pressure on the government in order to obtain the suspension of the gold standard on its own banknotes. The accusation was rejected with scorn by the same Ferrara who had, in his day, attacked Scialoja's policy. It is possible that the Banca Nazionale in 1866 had been worried about the fate of one important Genoese bank which would have found itself in a serious liquidity crisis.[11] If this was actually the case, as seems likely, even though very little is known about it, the suspension of the gold standard was instrumental in the success of the first important lending of last resort operation carried out in Italy. Between 1865 and 1866 the European finance markets were anything but tranquil and the future of the new Kingdom depended on Prussia: in this confused and uncertain climate a banking crisis would have been, to say the least, inopportune. If one considers the suspension of the gold standard to have played a part in avoiding this crisis, that is a further point in its favour.

On the whole, it is not very important to establish whether the suspension of the gold standard was dictated by internal and international financial circumstances, by the pressure of the Banca Nazionale or, as appears likely, by a mix of several factors. It is much more important to note that the measure, which was at the time accepted as the lesser evil, appears in perspective as anything but damaging to the Italy which was taking its first steps on the path towards modern economic growth.

Railways and public works

The Right believed in an indirect promotion of development mainly through the creation of that social overhead capital, which could not be left entirely to private enterprise either because of the amount of resources necessary for each single project, or because of the public interest involved (mainly of a strategic nature), or, finally, because of its technical or natural monopoly.

The railway was highly symbolic for the protagonists of the Risorgimento since it seemed to complete the process of political unification which in 1861 had received only political sanction.

Around 1860 the Italian railway network was about 2,000 kilometres, comparable with that of Spain, but inferior to that in Great Britain, Germany, and France.[12] However, substantial construction work was in progress: by the end of 1864 the network totalled about 3,400 kilometres. Of these, less than 600 were run directly by the state (especially in Piedmont) while the rest of the network was shared out among twenty-two private companies, some of which were extremely small.[13] In May 1865 the first important Italian Railway Act was approved in parliament. It sanctioned and regulated the regime of government concessions for the management of the railroads, sharing the main lines out among four large companies. The same Act reorganized the system of government contributions for the construction and running of the railways.

Between 1865 and 1876 another 3,857 kilometres were added, bringing the total network to nearly 8,000 which, immediately following political unification, were deemed necessary as the first requirement for the economic unification of the country. During the government of the Right an average 350 kilometres of new line were opened each year[14] and the base for a national network was created. In 1863 Naples was linked to Rome and the following year Bologna to Florence. In 1866 one could travel from the north as far down as Lecce and Naples. In the following years this expansion continued, even if between 1867 and 1876 the annual expenditure was on average a good third below that of 1861−5.

It should be remembered that the value of railway constructions, in the period 1861−76, represented half that of new public works.[15] Considerable attention was given to expanding the ports whose development was regulated by a law of 1865. The extension of arterial and provincial roads increased by about 15 per cent and that of secondary roads by around 30 per cent. A national telegraph service was created.

From a strictly quantitative point of view, the commitment of the governments of the Right to the creation of social overhead capital in Italy cannot be underestimated. In 1861 expenditure in public works represented 47 per cent of gross investment in the country as a whole. As already mentioned, this expenditure fell sharply after 1866. Despite this, ten years later, it still made up more than a quarter of the country's capital formation.

More complex is the evaluation of the productivity of these investments. On this point it is perhaps worth mentioning that during the last twenty years economic historians have dedicated considerable energy to attempting to measure the contribution given by the railways to modern economic growth.[16] Three main points have been singled out: the unification of the market (the line of research traditionally followed by historians), the 'social saving' of resources (capital and labour) in the national transport system, and the activation of demand to national industry.

As to the first two points, it should be said immediately that the inefficiency of the Italian railways soon became apparent. At the end of the 1870s an ad hoc inquiry committee[17] was appointed, but already during the parliamentary debate on the 1865 bill it had been clear that railway construction arose from a political rather than an economic need.[18] The operating results of the concessionary companies indirectly confirmed this judgement.[19] The construction of railroads in Italy was, on average, a more costly procedure than elsewhere, given the orographic characteristics of the peninsula. Running costs also remained very high. According to Fenoaltea these exceeded, at the end of the century, by about two-thirds those of France and Germany.[20] The abundant Italian labour was cheap but had 'exceptionally low productivity'[21] while energy prices were much higher than in north-western Europe. The network was often underutilized, especially during the years of the Right, before the completion of the secondary lines. The contribution to the unification of the market was, therefore, rather limited.

In the Italian context it is not very significant to calculate the 'social saving' of resources such as labour which were widely underutilized.[22] Research carried out so far indicates that railway construction produced limited effects on the demand for goods produced by industries:[23] this would appear particularly true for the fifteen years when the Right was in power.

Progress in industry

It has been seen how the existing estimates agree in attributing to the period 1865–76 a growth of per capita industrial production close to 1 per cent. This was slow, but not insignificant progress especially when considered in the light of both preceding and following trends. In fact, there are some scholars who see the growth of Italian industry as a 'process of long-term evolution'[24] characterized by a small but constant trend acceleration in manufacturing production.

In the course of modern economic growth heavy industry geared to the production of investment goods develops more rapidly than that of light industry sectors such as the food, textile, leather working, and timber industries. The latter sectors were the first to develop, starting from cottage industries, passing through an ambiguous process of 'proto-industrialization' and ending up with the modern factory system. This depends on conditions linked both to internal (priority given to primary needs) and international demand (the comparative advantages of a late developing country) and on the nature of supply. On this last point one should emphasize the capacity that some sectors have in integrating themselves with agricultural activity. In the Italian case, as in many other cases, the first phase of industrialization followed to a great extent, if not entirely, the fortunes of the textile sector. At the Unification, the quota of silk, cotton, and wool yarn and textiles although difficult to measure precisely, probably amounted to more than 30 per cent of total manufacturing production.

The silk industry, in these years, earned almost half the foreign currency coming into the country. Its comparative advantage lay in the low opportunity-cost of cocoon farming in an over-populated countryside in which the peasant had several idle days during the year. Almost all the mills were situated in rural areas and used surplus labour, mainly female, often in a discontinuous way. Wages could therefore be maintained at levels even lower than subsistence, given that for the worker this was an addition to the main family income deriving from agricultural activity. In 1866 there were 4,092 silk mills in Italy, most of them rather primitive: of these, in fact, only 386 had steam heated basins, all the others used direct heat.[25] Production underwent violent fluctuations connected to the ups and downs of cocoon harvests. Between 1863–5 and 1875–7 the production of drawn silk grew at an average annual rate of 1.4 per cent.[26] A large part of this drawn-silk output was exported as such, given that the productive capacity of the national weaving industry could only absorb a relatively small part of it.

The cotton industry did not enjoy a similar comparative advantage. All the raw material had to be imported (in the early 1860s, because of the American Civil War, prices rose steeply throughout Europe). The use of labour with a low opportunity-cost was not as easy. The many spindles and hand looms[27] were concentrated mainly in urban centres where wages were higher than in the country. This induced the introduction of labour saving investments: some firms were large and grew rapidly in these years. The Cotonificio Cantoni and the Manifatture di Cuorgnè became joint stock companies.[28] The Crespi took its first steps.[29] On the whole, judging by such an important index as the import of raw cotton, physical production seemed to grow at a very high rate in this period (close to 8 per cent a year between 1861–3 and 1875–7).[30] In one decade (1867–77) the number of spindles in operation increased from 450,000 to 800,000; exceeding those in Belgium, a small but industrialized country which at the Unification surpassed Italy.[31] This appears due exclusively to the growth in domestic demand given the insignificant quantity of cotton textiles exported by Italy up to the mid-1890s.

The growth of wool production appears much smaller, judging from the apparent consumption of raw materials: only 1.1 per cent a year in the period of the Right. However, this industry was qualitatively important since it included some of the most advanced and most well-organized factories in the country.[32] The textile panorama is completed by the linen and hemp industries the growth of which is difficult to quantify at the present state of our knowledge.

The food industry was 'still based on a myriad of mills (often using only animal power) and of small wine workshops of an artisan nature: the only exception being the development of the preserves and sugar refining sectors, monopolized to a great extent by Cirio and by the Società Ligure Lombarda, which opened in Genoa in 1871.'[33]

As to the sectors which in the 1860s and 1870s could be considered the most modern, the statistics for these years, however uncertain and incomplete, lead one to think that output around 1860 was limited and the growth rate low. Production and consumption of pig-iron are approximate but significant indicators of the progress made by heavy industry in this period (see Table 7.1).

The situation in the engineering sector was very varied: at any rate we know little about its progress, imports of iron and steel rose from 69,000 tonnes (average 1861–3) to 117,400 at the time the Right fell from power (average 1875–7).[34] Apparent consumption

Table 7.1 Output of pig iron 1861–75 (Italy in 1861 = 1)

	Italy	*U.K.*	*Germany*	*France*	*Belgium*	*Austria*	*Russia*
1861	1	140	22	33	12	9	12
1875	1.1	239	65	53	20	11	16
average growth rate p.a. (1861–75)	0.5	3.7	7.5	2.7	3.7	1.8	1.9

Source: B.R. Mitchell, *European Historical Statistics 1750–1970*, London: Macmillan, 1975, pp. 216–19.

of this important input in the engineering industry grew at an average annual rate of 3.8 per cent.[35] The other information we possess is asystematic and descriptive. It leads one to think, however, that Italian engineering production suffered, in the first years after the Unification, from an overall technical backwardness. Romeo notes, for example, that Italian shipbuilding, which showed an increase between 1861 and 1875, was still based to a large extent on sailing ships and that when these could no longer compete with steam production fell rapidly.[36] Another indication of the relative backwardness of Italy's engineering industry lies in the already mentioned fact that a large part of the demand created by the railways had to be met by foreign products: of the 806 locomotives put into service by the three leading Italian railway companies between 1861 and 1874, only 110 were of national manufacture; produced mainly by the Ansaldo works in Sampierdarena and those in Pietrarsa near Naples.[37]

As to the chemical industry – the other large sector destined to become very important in Italy's modern economic growth – there are systematic statistics available only from the 1890s onwards. However, the few monographs and inquiries of the time show that this industry was almost non-existent. In the early 1870s, the young engineer Giovanni Battista Pirelli founded the first rubber-processing factory, but the development of this firm, and of the industry as a whole, would take place only in successive decades with the production of insulating materials, undersea cables, and, later, tyres for motor vehicles.

The Right and economic development: an overview

The fact that many exponents of the Right belonged to the landed class and were fervent free traders lies behind the view that the attitude of this restricted elite of moderates was constantly biased against industry and, therefore, had a negative influence on modern economic growth. Thus, the Right has been described as generally anti-industrialist in attitude and Castronovo maintains that 'Italian industry would have had great difficulty in coming out of the blind alley to which free-tradist inadequacy had condemned it.'[38] The first to complain of this state of affairs, after the Unification, were the southern industrialists who felt they were being damaged by the liberal tariff imposed on the country by the agrarian interests in the north.

Distinction should be made between the Right's overall ideology and its ability to understand the problems of modern economic growth, and the more specific question of its attitude towards customs laws. It must be remembered that not even the Right was a homogeneous group as far as ideology and economic interests were concerned. Cavour, as has been seen, certainly did not have an Arcadian vision of economic development. Sella was committed to promoting conditions favourable for the growth of industrial production;[39] he had a clear vision of the importance and role of accumulation and technical progress. His insistence on achieving a balanced budget, anything but peacefully accepted, was based on the awareness of the crowding-out effect of public debt.[40] The preference of many on the Right for unification of note issue and state running of the railways can be explained in part by their aversion to financial rent and their desire that the state be a more active promotor of development.

At the same time, one must recall that

> there existed a diffidence common to the majority of the political class both of the Left and Right . . . towards the more obvious manifestations of capitalism, lest class struggle arise again. All Cavour's successors, either Left or Right, (with the exception of Sella), were mere provincials when compared to the master and his consistent capitalist ideology.[41]

Furthermore, this diffidence was also typical of the Catholic leaders, for the moment excluded from active politics, but very much present with many followers and much influence, especially among the peasants. At the first Catholic congress, held in Venice in 1874, both modern society and the liberal revolution were denounced as overturning 'relations between city and countryside to the disadvantage of agricultural populations [creating] the scourge of urbanism, the real "mark of Cain".'[42]

A large number of those who led the government or influenced social behaviour showed, during the 1860s and 1870s, caution, diffidence or open hostility towards modern economic growth. This should come as no surprise given that one of its features is that of subverting existing relations between productive and social groups and of creating drastically different life-styles from those prevalent in a traditional static society. This was not an exceptional situation: generally speaking, modern economic growth is favoured by an ideology homogeneous to it, but this becomes dominant only with the reinforcement of growth itself, the first phases of which often take place in a vicious circle similar to that in which Italy was also trapped.

The public inquiry on the conditions of industry

In the winter of 1869–70 official mention was made for the first time in Parliament of setting up an inquiry into Italian industry. The declared objective was that of collecting material for a revision of customs treaties. In fact, many industrialists believed that free trade had been introduced too rapidly in the early 1860s.

The Inquiry Committee met for the first time in 1870 under the chairmanship of Antonio Scialoja. Luigi Luzzatti – who was to chair the parliamentary commission for the Customs Act of 1887 – took part, as did the wool industrialist Alessandro Rossi.[43] The latter is a personality of some note in Italian industrial history: he is credited with having made the voices of the entrepreneurs heard, not without a certain authority, in the post-Unification political debate. His views were essentially different from those of the governing moderate Right and from those of the Catholic movement then just beginning to organize itself. Rossi is, therefore, considered by some historians as the first to understand the needs of Italian economic development. He asked openly that the state, given Italy's backwardness, promote conditions which would make businesses more competitive. For that to happen, at least in the home market, it was necessary to abandon the dogmatic free-tradism of the early post-Unification years, to make the customs a tool of development. The Inquiry lasted for four years. The industrialists provided much information on conditions in Italian manufacturing. However, the prime objective was not information. The Inquiry made producers more aware of the need to organize themselves and led them to ask for the simplest measure in their favour: customs protection. Once the findings had been published, the Inquiry served as a pressure tool to obtain greater government attention for the problems facing industry. We shall see how the political climate changed, after 1876, as Rossi and the promotors of the Inquiry had wished; however, the change was not without its ambiguities – unscrupulously taken for granted by the pragmatism of the industrialists' leader – and was both slow and contradictory as far as economic policy was concerned.

Chapter eight

The contradictions of the 1880s

Agricultural slump and industrial development

The financial crisis of 1873, which spread from Berlin to other important European stock markets, marked the beginning of that 'great depression' which, according to many scholars, lasted for the following two decades in most of the European economies. The phenomenon appears quite clear if one observes the trend of prices, almost universally in decline. Less apparent was the 'depression' in real levels of economic activity. The indices of industrial production, however, continued their long-term growth.[1] National income also grew in Europe during this period, although probably at a slightly lower rate than that in the period 1849–73. The depression mainly concerned cereal cultivation, hit by the competition from the American prairies which had been opened to European markets by the second wave of railway investment following the Civil War. Given both the economic and political importance of the agricultural producers, free trade soon gave way to a protectionist mood almost everywhere in Europe: import duties began to protect the domestic production of grain. An agreement with industrial interests and, therefore, more or less inefficient tariff compromises were made necessary and were ultimately extended to sectors other than cereal cultivation.

In this context, the Italian situation, on the whole, does not appear, very different from that in the rest of Europe. The peculiarity of the Italian case can, perhaps, be seen in the fact that a particularly serious agricultural crisis was accompanied by exceptionally flourishing industrial production.

Gross agricultural product in 1887 was virtually the same as in 1876. In terms of per capita product, therefore, the situation had been deteriorating. Over the same period, the ISTAT–Fuà index of industrial production grew by 1.2 per cent per annum, while the Fenoaltea index shows an annual increase of 5.4. If we confine ourselves to the period 1880–7 the two rates are equal to 3.4 and 7.5 respectively. In spite of the large gap between the two estimates, in both cases the industrial situation is in marked contrast to the agricultural slump.

The agricultural crisis

The slump in agricultural production was closely linked to the wheat harvests which fell from 38.6 million quintals per annum to an average of 32.6 million from 1875–7 to 1886–8. In the same period domestic wholesale prices for soft wheat fell by about 28 per cent, despite the introduction of import duties.[2] It is not difficult, therefore, to conclude that an exogenous fall in prices, due to overseas competition which became particularly strong from 1880 onwards, was at the root of the sharp fall in production due to the fact that a considerable amount of marginal acreage devoted to wheat cultivation became uncompetitive.

A fall in the yield per hectare has also been noted.[3] If such was the case, it can be explained by the fact that during the agricultural crisis the movement in relative prices made it worthwhile for some farmers to reallocate their best land to alternative crops such as forage, potatoes, hemp, and rice in the Po valley and citrus fruit, vines, and olives in the south. In fact, the decline in wheat and other types of cereal cultivation was accompanied by a not inconsiderable increase in sugar-beet, citrus fruit, oil, and wine production.[4] This being the case, one may argue that the crisis forced Italian agriculture to reallocate its resources in such a way as to make better use of the abundant farm labour, by introducing crops which were more labour intensive than wheat cultivation.

However, this in no way means that the agricultural crisis was without negative effects, both in terms of welfare and, in the medium term, on the time pattern of modern economic growth. Its overall impact, however, has not been fully assessed so far.

One of the macroeconomic manifestations of this crisis was the increase in cereal imports[5] which, however, did not prevent an overall fall in per capita food consumption:[6] It is not difficult to imagine what this meant for the population in an economy already close to subsistence level.

The crisis hit hardest 'in northern Italy because its agriculture was quite well inserted in the market.'[7] The price of hard wheat, a typical southern product, fell less than that of soft wheat. As to the producers, it has been noted that 'the small holding, precisely because it was less devoted to cereal cultivation and more to arboriculture was not hit so badly or, at any rate, reacted better to the crisis – at least until the outbreak of the trade war with France (1887–90).'[8]

The growth of industry

As already noted, during the agricultural crisis there was a flowering of industrial production, at least in the period 1880–7.[9] The only available breakdowns by individual industries are those of Gerschenkron.[10] They highlight how this rapid development is attributable mainly to the metal-making, chemical, and engineering sectors. The textile industry seemed to continue the long trend acceleration which had started after 1848, while the food processing industry felt the effects of the agricultural slump.

The history of metal-making was marked by the foundation, in 1884, of the Terni steel works:[11] steel production which, until 1885, oscillated between 3–4 thousand tonnes a year, leapt to 157,000 tonnes in 1889.[12] These were still very small amounts compared to the 3 million tonnes produced in the United Kingdom, 2 million in Germany and even to the 600,000 produced in France. However, the leap forward in the three-year period was such as to influence the industrial index considerably. The doubling of iron production between 1880 and 1889 was even more significant in that it was not linked to the rise of one single firm.[13]

In the 1880s, the engineering industry saw the rise of firms destined to play key roles: Franco Tosi (1882) and Breda (1886). From the beginning the latter played an important part in the import–substitution of locomotives. Those made in Italy[14] in the period 1885–90 covered about 40 per cent of total demand,[15] while 'already in 1881 imports of railway wagons and carriages were the exception.'[16] However, the still backward structure of the sector must not be forgotten: of the estimated 218,000 workers in 1881 145,000 were blacksmiths. According to Warglien, however,[17] Italian production of machinery grew at an average annual rate of 14.6 per cent in the period 1881–7. Net imports also rose rapidly: national industry started from a very restricted base and was characterized by a rather rigid supply curve typical of backward countries so that the engineering sector was unable to meet the strong demand for investment goods of the 1880s.

There is very little quantitative information available for the chemical industry – also in expansion according to Gerschenkron. Production of sulphuric acid has been estimated at 50,000 tonnes in 1890 as against the 11,000 in 1880.[18] In this case, too, the level reached by Italy lagged far behind that of the United Kingdom

(900,000 tonnes) and Germany (400,000 tonnes), but the growth rate of 16.3 per cent per annum appears exceptionally good.

Cotton production was rather dynamic judging by the increase in raw cotton consumption (7.8 per cent a year between 1881 and 1887). It should be noted that this industry, at least as far as yarn is concerned, developed during the 1880s due to an import substitution process, induced by the tariff of 1878.

On the whole, the manufacturing sector was characterized by the rapid growth of 'new' industries producing mainly investment or intermediate goods, which began with very low production levels; by the steady development of fairly well-established sectors which were now replacing previously imported goods, and by a limited growth in the more traditional sectors tied to agriculture (silk, and particularly foodstuffs).

However, development was not limited to manufacturing: the value added of the construction industry grew, between 1876 and 1887, by 7.2 per cent a year according to the ISTAT–Fuà estimates. Public works contributed considerably to this growth. The expansion in private building was linked, more or less directly, to state intervention: one need only mention the slum clearance projects in Naples and the work carried out in Rome to make the urban structure suitable for the requirements of a capital city.

Financial intermediation and development

At the time of Italy's political unification the banks of issue were, in fact, the only credit institutions whose dimensions and operative capacity significantly transcended provincial limits.[19] They met the demand for commercial and industrial credit (that is, medium- and long-term credit). This state of affairs derived from the fact that the Italian financial was extremely limited, apart from that market for state bonds. Industrial capital came therefore from family fortunes and from the long-established domestic and foreign finance houses. However, intermediaries slowly began to emerge. As already mentioned, in 1863 the Péreire brothers, engaged in a dispute of European dimensions between their Crédit Mobilier and the House of Rothschild, founded the Società Generale di Credito Mobiliare Italiano which remained 'for a long time modelled on the realizations' of the two tenacious Saint-Simonian financiers and which 'was more similar to a modern finance house than to a bank'.[20] In this context one should also mention the Banca Tiberina: 'much more than just a simple credit institution, committed as it was to typical building operations',[21] and the Banca di

Torino 'similar in more ways than one to a holding company.'[22] This similarity was present, though to a lesser degree, in many of the credit institutions, including even the small local co-operative banks (Banche Popolari).[23]

The Italian merchant banks remained small in size. Their assets consisted mainly in a small amount of industrial and railway securities not easy to liquidate.[24]

During the early 1880s, demand for real investment rose considerably: that in machinery and means of transport grew, between 1879 and 1887, by almost 10 per cent a year in real terms, thus creating a demand for financial intermediation services. The growth rate of the latter reached its peak in the period 1875–87 (see Table 3.1: p. 24); the weight of banking intermediaries on the total, however, remained almost unchanged. The various categories of banks developed in a dynamic and balanced way: even the growth of the Savings and Co-operative Banks should not be underestimated. In 1887 these collected together about 30 per cent of the total liabilities of the banking intermediaries (as against the 21 per cent of ten years earlier). The banks of issue, however, retained a considerable quantitative importance, while the commercial banks were the most dynamic segment of the credit sector in this period. It will be seen how this dynamism led to overtrading and financial instability ultimately producing a most serious crisis in the whole credit system.[25] What interests us now is the role played by the financial intermediation system in the manufacturing and construction boom of the 1880s.

Around 1878 there were signs of a reawakening in the stock markets while the expansion of commercial banks speeded up. The assets of the latter grew at an average rate of 6.2 per cent in the period 1877–82. The volume of discounts granted by the banks of issue also increased considerably. The banks intensified their investments in transport (apart from the railways with which they already had strong ties) and construction industries. This interest was all the more apparent, as Warglien notes,[26] in that it came about in a context of a restrictive monetary policy enacted to about the return to the gold standard. After 1883 the expansion of credit was also supported by net capital imports favoured by the new monetary stability and by the high interest rates maintained in order to defend it.

Between 1882 and 1887 bank lending increased even more rapidly: that of the commercial banks grew by 15 per cent per annum. Credit was mainly given to the 'modern' sectors in expansion. It should be noted, however, that the great profit-making opportunities for the banks opened up in the building sector in which normal industrial profits were augmented by speculation. These oppotunities derived from the rapid increases in the value of building sites in expanding cities – mainly Rome, but also Turin, Milan, and Naples.

On the whole, the financial structure of businesses during this first period of acceleration of industrial production was typical of a late nineteenth century backward country. Using Warglien's analysis[27] of the balance-sheets of joint-stock companies, this structure can be summarized as follows. First, the businesses in an already fairly well-developed sector, which had medium to small productive units (e.g. the textile sector) self-financed not only their fixed investment but also inventory, and restored to external finance only for commercial credit. Second, on the contrary, firms in the more 'modern' rapidly expanding sectors (the steel, engineering, chemical, and sugar industries) tended to finance fixed investments with short-term bank loans. The same was true of building and tramline companies. Third, there were cases of what would nowadays be defined as holding companies, which used bank loans not only to finance plant and equipment but also to buy shareholdings in other companies: this is an interesting example of financial capitalism arising from and founded on credit. Finally, most large transport firms (especially in the railway and maritime sectors) financed their large capital requirements by bond issues (sometimes with state guarantees). The banks favoured the placement of such bonds and held part of them in their own portfolios. Apart from the important case of the older industrial sectors, it is clear that the banks' intermediation was probably an important element in the investment boom of the 1880s. This type of finance, however, increased both the fragility of the system and the dangers of a recession of considerable dimensions and duration.

Fiscal policy

The debate on state intervention in the economy was at the centre of the political struggle between 1875 and 1876 and it culminated in the 'parliamentary revolution' which brought the Left to power. The most hotly-debated issues were railways concessions and customs legislation. On the first of these points, part of the Right held that private companies had not provided adequate services, and favoured direct running of railways by the state on the expiry of the concession. The arguments of Minghetti, Sella, and Spaventa in favour of this solution were both contingent and a matter of principle. On a practical level they revealed the inefficiency of a service requiring burdensome state contributions;

on a theoretical level they claimed that the railways were almost a natural monopoly and should, therefore, be run by the state in the public interest, all the more so because the railways would never have been built without the all-important aid of public finance. The government signed two important contracts for the surrender of the networks to the state, but these were not ratified by parliament owing to the fall, on 18 March 1876, of the last government of the Right.

The Left, which formed the successive governments, was a composite group. The experience of conspiracy and revolution which united many of its exponents became radicalism which, as far as economic policy was concerned meant – before gaining power – adherence to the purest liberal principles. They were therefore ideologically opposed to the choices of the Right as far as railways and banking were concerned. Once in power, however, the Left had to tone down its radicalism both because of the objective complexity of the problems to be faced and the political need to maintain equilibrium between the various groups represented in the government.

The railways issue provides a good case in point. A parliamentary committee of inquiry was formed in 1878 and ended its work three years later with a report in favour of private running of the railways. In the meantime, however, the state, which already ran the Northern Italian network on the basis of the contract signed in 1875, acquired (1880) the property of the *Ferrovie Romane* which had accumulated large budget deficits. The proposal, in 1883, of a Bill to reorganize the network provoked a government crisis. The industrialists supported state-run railways which, in their opinion, would mean lower transport costs.[28] The railway contracts approved by parliament on 27 April 1885 were a compromise between the supporters of total privatization and those in favour of state running. These contracts made provisions for private running of state-held lines. The main concessionaries were reduced to three. This made a second wave of railway construction easier. This regarded mainly secondary lines which probably provided higher social savings than the main lines created by the Right outside the Po valley.[29] In these years the state did not limit itself to the creation of social overhead capital: direct support was also given to the industries held to be indispensable for defence purposes and, in general, for the development of the country and which required too high a fixed investment threshold for the autonomous initiative of the timid Italian capitalist. The creation of the Terni works in 1884 forged the first links between industry, finance, and state, which were to be an important feature of Italy's economic development.

As to the question of tariffs, the Left soon had to revise its position of radical free-tradism.

Monetary and fiscal policies in the early years of the Left were a continuation of those of previous governments, which had aimed at gradual reduction of the deficit and return to the gold standard. In 1879 the state budget was almost balanced. Deficits remained fairly contained until 1885. The Minister of Finance for almost all this period was Antonio Magliani:[30] his fiscal policy reflected the political contradictions with which the Left was struggling. On the one hand it tried to respect orthodox financial canons so that there would be no risk of nostalgia for the Right's rigorous pursual of a balanced budget. On the other hand, the government had to redress the balance of the highly regressive fiscal policy inherited from the Right,[31] increase expenditure on defence and, by giving generously to single groups or areas, smooth over difficulties in the precarious politico-parliamentary alliances then supporting the ruling coalitions. Actual revenue during the 1880s remained at around 12 to 13 per cent of national income while expenditure tended to rise more rapidly, especially towards the end of the decade: from 1886 on, the state budget deficit grew in absolute value as well as a share of national income.

The return to the gold standard

Coming off the gold standard, justified to the public in 1866 because of the war, was felt as a national shame by many Italian politicians. Both Right and Left made the return to the gold standard one of the main objectives of monetary policy. Magliani was therefore able to get a law passed, almost unanimously, in April 1881, which regulated the return to metal payments.[32] This law made provision for the issue of a loan, to be subscribed in gold, in order to guarantee adequate and credible reserves and thus discourage speculation. The placing of 644 million Italian Consols was guaranteed by the Baring and Hambro groups, by the French Banque d'Escompte and by the Banca Nazionale del Regno, together with the Credito Mobiliare. The return to payments in gold was fixed for April 1883.

The political tension with France when the return to the gold standard came about made the operation less easy especially because of the fall in the price of Italian Consols on the Paris Stock Exchange, perhaps caused by the Rothschilds, which led many Italians to take advantage of the occasion in order to buy Consols abroad, thus causing a sudden outflow of gold reserves from the country. Apart from this, operations proceeded in an orderly fashion: in 1883 the expected run on gold, which many had forecast, did not actually come about. Thus, this measure, desired for mainly political reasons, did not create important problems of a technical nature in the short term.[33]

Despite the success of the operation, however, its long-term effects were probably less favourable. In this case, too, it is only possible to advance hypotheses, given the lack of an *ad hoc* quantitative analysis. It seems likely that the fragility of the banking system was increased by the fact that ideological preconceptions and vested interests prevented a thorough reform of the banks of issue. As early as 1881 Minghetti had expressed concern about the possible effects of a return to the gold standard on the Tuscan and Roman banks.[34] The fact that their operations were confined to a local level made the necessary replacement of currency circulation with deposits more difficult for them than for the larger banks. The way in which the return to gold came about increased their already serious liquidity problems so that it seems likely that the seeds of the crisis, which was to explode with such violence at the end of the century, were planted in this particular period.

As far as foreign trade and domestic production are concerned, the revaluation of the external value of the lira which followed the return to the gold standard seems not to have had important effects either one way or another. The exchange rate of the lira appreciated, with respect to the end of the 1870s, by about 10 per cent between 1882 and 1886 when it began to slide down again.[35] In 1883–4 the domestic prices tended to compensate for the revaluation of the lira with a fall greater than that in the leading European countries.[36] The immediate effect on the balance of trade can only have been small: the increasing deficit must, therefore, be attributed to other causes and in particular to the greater competitiveness of American wheat and to the investment boom in the presence of a considerable rigidity in the domestic supply of technically advanced machinery. This boom and the growth of GDP indicate, on the other hand, that the fall in prices did not produce relevant deflationary effects. After 1885 Italian prices, compared to those at the beginning of the decade, remained at higher levels than those in France and England and the devaluation of the exchange rate in the following year was not able to bring purchasing power back to its 1880 level. One may argue therefore that the parity set for the return to the gold standard was too high. Capital imports were favoured at the expense of the trade balance. This must be emphasized, in the light of the financial instability generated by the inflow of short-term foreign capital (see Chapter nine).

The tariffs of 1876 and 1887

The practical result of the industrial inquiry was to highlight how widespread among businessmen was the request for state support in the form of higher import duties, justified by an 'infant industry' argument. The fact that Depretis led his 'parliamentary revolution' waving the banner of unmitigated free trade did not discourage the supporters, led by Alessandro Rossi, of higher protection for domestic goods. It is interesting to note that

> the role played by the representatives of the financial aristocracy in determining the fall of the Right is one of the few cases in the history of the Italian state in which the dominant economic forces had directly taken the initiative on a political ground. But it is very difficult to suppose that the Tuscan members of parliament – the leading representatives of this aristocracy – would have taken the initiative had they not known that a similar anti-ministerial initiative was more than ripe among members from the South.[37]

If the Italian financiers, and the Tuscan ones in particular, favoured free trade it was also true, in practice, that their *laissez-faire* was mostly concerned with maintaining the existing issuing privileges to the banks of issue. In order to safeguard the freedom of the latter they were prepared to concede something to the 'southern deputation' whose agricultural interests had been hard hit by the fall in cereal prices, and to the group of industrialists who invoked the revision of the general tariff and who had also played a part in Depretis' election. The tariff law passed by the Cairoli government in 1878[38] was an example of the more or less transformist compromises to which the leaders of the Left had to submit in order to keep their heterogenous majority united.

The new tariff law replaced the previous *ad valorem* duties with specific ones, easier to collect. The tariff was the result of a compromise which the advocates of free trade later defined as *pactum sceleris* (meaning an agreement to do something immoral or illegal). The financial circles accepted the tariff in exchange for the maintenance of the existing regime regarding the banks of issue and the industrialists granted a duty on cereals to the southern agriculturalists,[39] which corresponded to 3.1 per cent of the average value of wheat in 1879, and to 6.4 per cent in 1887.[40] As to industrial products, protection was granted mostly to already fairly developed industries with a parliamentary lobby. The textile sector was especially favoured. The wool, cotton, jute, and silk industries benefited from legislation in the form of duties which varied from

10 to 40 per cent. The tariff reform, therefore, was a missed opportunity to stimulate the more promising of the 'new' industries and, in particular, engineering. The Italian case was further proof of the political difficulty implied in implementing protection of infant industry.

The 1878 tariff was soon overtaken by two important events: the continuance of the fall in prices and the beginnings, with state support, of a modern steel industry which very soon acquired considerable political weight. From 1882 there had been talk of revising the tariff made less protective by the customs treaties of 1878 with Austria and of 1881 with France.[41]

In November 1882 Magliani presented a bill containing several amendments to the tariff law. This was passed the following July together with Luzzatti's proposal for setting up an Inquiry Committee to look into further modifications of customs regulations. It is interesting to note that, while the report drafted by Ellena in 1886 on the industrial problem advocated increased protectionism, Lampertico and Miraglia, reporting on agriculture, did not believe in the virtues of further protectionist action. But their opinion did not reflect that of the prevailing landed interests: under the pressure of falling international prices even liberal landlords became advocates of protectionism.[42]

In July 1887 Parliament approved a new tariff law.[43] The short debate which preceded the vote makes instructive reading for those interested in the politics of the clientele system. The text of the bill granted the requests of large pressure groups – grain growers, textile, and steel industry – which had kept a low profile during the discussion, which was monopolized by a myriad of speeches and amendments proposed, often with success, by little-known members from the provinces whose only objective consisted in obtaining a shower of customs duties for industries – or rather, firms, even though these were not named – which had some importance in their constituencies. The result of these pressures was a less rational law, in terms of effective protection, compared to the original project presented in the Chamber. Thus several unimportant petty interests were taken into consideration, while yet again the demands of the most promising infant industries, which in more developed countries were producing that wave of innovations which lead one to speak of a 'second industrial revolution', were ignored. One need only have looked to Germany to understand, for example, the strategic importance of the progress made by the chemical industry.

The tariff was characterized above all by an increase in the duty on wheat from 1.4 to 3 lire per quintal, rising in 1885 to 5 lire[44] equivalent to about 25 per cent of the c.i.f. (cost, insurance, freight) value of imported wheat. A second important characteristic of the new tariff lay in the treatment reserved for the cotton industry in which spinning was privileged over weaving. It can be calulated that the duty on yarn was, on average, equal to 27 per cent *ad valorem*, while textiles were covered only with a duty of 7 per cent which implied little or even negative effective protection.[45] This 'irrationality' of the tariff was a sign of the inability of a considerable part of the Italian industrial bourgeoisie to unite in order to safeguard common long-term interests. The relatively restricted wool sector which had a more compact and far-sighted leadership, was able to obtain a 'rational' tariff treatment with effective protection lower but positive for both spinning and weaving. A third characteristic element of this tariff lay in the high import duty for cast-iron and steel, as compared to the much more moderate one granted to the main products of engineering, which ended up with an effective protection close to zero.[46]

Chapter nine

A decade of crisis: 1887–96

Political changes and economic crisis

The widespread depression in industrial production and investment, which culminated in a dangerous financial crisis, led Gino Luzzatto, the most respected Italian economic historian, to define the years 1889–94 as 'the blackest for the new Kingdom's economy.'[1]

The first indications of crisis appeared in 1887–8 and coincided with the political turning-point which followed the death of Depretis in July 1887. A revival in production was visible only around 1894–5. Investments rose again only after 1896. If these were indeed the 'blackest years' – for reasons more important than the cyclical downturn in production – the whole period when Crispi was in power appears to the economic historian as one profound and prolonged crisis. Almost as if to highlight the difficulties at home and abroad, this period lies between two unfortunate military episodes at Dogali and Adua, in East Africa. Relatively unimportant in themselves, such episodes reveal the ingenuous improvisation of late Italian imperialism and symbolize to a certain extent the salient political features of the time: authoritarianism at home and restless daring abroad. The economic crisis, which reached its peak in 1893, was intertwined with a political situation which saw a fierce struggle in government circles and, at the same time, the spread of discontent and unrest among the populace.

The political protagonist of these years was Francesco Crispi, Minister of Home Affairs in the eighth Depretis cabinet formed in April 1887, Prime Minister from August of the same year until February 1891, and again from December 1893 to March 1896. The interval between his two mandates was covered, after Rudinì, by the first Giolitti government whose action and programming were already indicative of the political tendencies which were to emerge in the following decade, during what is called 'the Age of Giolitti'.

In 1893, when the crisis and banking scandals were at their peak, the battle was on between Crispi and Giolitti and would see the victory of the former.[2]

For the purposes of an economic analysis of the period one should bear in mind the elements of continuity and novelty present in the political life of the country. These can be summarized as follows:

Transformism continued . . . but with a widened base, not only in parliament but also in the country since at this moment a new power block was formed which had its propulsive nucleus in the alliance between the more conservative agricultural interests and industry. In June and July 1887 parliament rapidly and easily approved the increase in the duty on grain and the new protectionist customs tariff. . . . This coalition of interests was at the base of the widened transformism, which, in its turn, was one of the elements which made Crispi's authoritarian policy possible.[3]

Many have seen this alliance as the indirect cause of the economic difficulties of the time, which had been sparked off by a trade war with France,[4] provoked both by the difficulties in negotiating a new trade treaty and by the political differences between the two countries deriving from the Italo–German military pact, accompanied by the renewal of the Triple Alliance along explicitly anti-French lines, as well as by Italy's ambitions in the Mediterranean.

The effects of the trade war cannot easily be distinguished from those produced, especially on Italian agriculture, by the tariff barriers erected by all the European countries during this period, nor from those caused by the fall in the levels of activity (and, consequently, in imports) which occurred in some countries during the final phase of the 'great depression'. In general, however, it is not difficult to advance the hypothesis that international economic difficulties (in 1890 there was a serious financial crisis in London) and the uncertainty generated by Crispi's policy together with social tension all contributed to the creation of unfavourable expectations especially as regards financial investments. All these factors, together with the 'fragility' of the system and the excess of investments from 1882–7, help in explaining the seriousness of this crisis.

Trade cycle and economic policy

The indices of both Gerschenkron and Fenoaltea show a reversal of industrial production cycle around 1888. Both indices decrease until 1892 when they slowly begin to rise once again. For Gerschenkron the 1888 production level was reached again in 1896, while for Fenoaltea this took place in 1898. Far less pronounced, as always happens, was the business cycle in agriculture. This fact, and the far less pronounced fall in the ISTAT index of industrial production than in the two indices just mentioned, explain the limited drop in GDP, according to existing estimates. National income would fall only in 1889 (− 3.2 per cent), in 1892 (− 3.8 per cent) and in 1895 (− 1.1 per cent). The level of national income in 1889–95 was higher by an average of 2 per cent than that in 1886–8.

On the whole, therefore, if we accept the existing estimates, it is likely that the 'blackest years' were not seen as such by the great mass of Italians, at least as far as standard of living was concerned. This is not to say, however, that important parts of the population and large areas of the country may not have suffered reductions in income such as to justify either the discontent or even the open revolt seen in these years, especially in the south. The protest, however, seemed linked to the exasperation at the lack of solutions for age-old problems; at unkept promises, and at the continuing difficulties in agriculture. It was not by chance that Giolitti, who knew Italian society inside out, hinged his first government's programme (May 1892–December 1893) not so much on monetary policy as on a reform of the Italian tax system which he condemned as 'regressive'.

At first sight, the budgetary policy carried out during the crisis does not appear to be the most suitable to support aggregate demand. Deficit spending reached its highest level in 1889, when it was equal to 4 per cent of GDP. It was steadily reduced thereafter, falling to 1 per cent in 1895 and then turning into the budget surpluses which were to characterize the 'Age of Giolitti' until the war in Libya. Between 1888 and 1896 money supply remained more or less stable. Given the fact that the balance of payments on current account balanced in 1891 and then had considerable surpluses one cannot but think that an expansionary fiscal and monetary policy would have cushioned the fall of industrial production and accelerated the reversal of the trade cycle. However, this initial impression must be qualified. First of all it should be recognized that, at the peak of the boom, budget deficit, public debt, and foreign payments deficit were sizeable and could

An economic history of Liberal Italy

not easily be increased. An increase in foreign debt was out of the question, given the 'wide discredit' of Italian finance in international circles and the continuing crisis in economic relations with Paris where the most substantial quotas of Italian foreign debt had traditionally been held. For these reasons the implementation of an adequate policy for balancing the budget could no longer be postponed. In fact, both the Rudinì and Giolitti governments explicitly proposed balancing the state budget, mainly through a more careful expenditure policy. As to monetary policy – probably more restrictive than the statistics relative to money supply indicate, owing to the fall in the banks' liquidity – it should be said that this too moved in a context of serious financial disorder largely deriving from the 'easy money' policy of the previous years. After 1887 there was a strong outflow of foreign capital with a consequent depreciation of exchange rates despite the improvement in current accounts, which resulted in high interest rates.

Trade cycle and finance

Contemporaries and historians alike have attributed the small investment boom at the beginning of the 1880s to the monetary effects of the return to the gold standard in 1883.[5] The international loan negotiated for the occasion, by increasing the reserves of the banks of issue produced an increase in money supply and in the banks' liquidity which continued to be sustained by an inflow of foreign capital. Easy credit produced a deterioration in the banks' portfolios. Their assets became more risky due to their increasingly speculative nature in the second half of the decade.

Among other things, these conditions allowed the large banks to finance long-term fixed investments (e.g. in the Terni steel works and in the construction industry). The engineering, metal-making, and chemical industries were the main sectors demanding credit for new factories, as indeed were some parts of the food processing industry.[6] The resulting structure of the banks' portfolios and of some financial houses, such as Breda and Cirio, increased the fragility of the financial system.

During the boom of the 1880s, the rigidity of domestic supply of industrial goods, especially investments, and the low price of Russian and American cereals (before the 1887 tariff) produced large and growing deficits in the balance of trade which were compensated for by the inflow of short-term foreign capital. The crisis of 1887 saw the withdrawal of foreign capital, the devaluation of the exchange rate, the outflow of metal reserves and the consequent reduction in the liquidity of the system.[7]

After 1885 the speculative behaviour of the leading banks, including the banks of issue, became more apparent. The growth of the ratio of deposits to capital and reserves was accompanied by a fall in the liquidity ratio. In particular, banks such as the Credito Mobilare, the Banca Generale, the Banca Tiberina as well as the Banca Romana were largely supplying credit to investments connected with the construction boom, above all in Rome, but also in Turin and Naples. This activity led, until 1887, to rises in the value of buildings and urban land values which allowed high returns on capital both for the operators and for the credit firms. Property prices reached their peak in the early months of 1887.[8] Then the tendency reversed:

> The crisis in the construction industry, which began in Rome and Naples and the accompanying crisis in some of the large metal-making industries, starting with Terni, created serious difficulties not only for the banks most closely linked to those firms (such as the Banca Tiberina, the Società dell'Esquilino, and the Banco di Sconto e Sete), but also to the two largest Italian banks, that is to the Banca Generale and the Società Generale di Credito Mobiliare.[9]

In other words, the losses made by the construction firms were transferred to the banks which had been in the front line of speculation. Credit of last resort from the banks of issue became necessary. At considerable cost the banking system was stabilized for another two or three years.

The reversal of the trend in credit supply from the second half of 1887 onwards, was reflected in that of industrial investments. The existing series of total net investments fell by 65 per cent between 1887 and 1892, remained at a very low level in the following three years, and fell again by 32 per cent between 1895 and 1897 when a slow revival took place (the 1887 value was reached again only at the beginning of 1905). This cycle was the result of very different behaviour in various sectors.

Apparent machinery consumption[10] – a rough indicator of investment in the manufacturing industry consisting of domestic production plus net imports – fell by 42 per cent between 1889 and 1892. This too was the result of different behaviour in individual sectors, which, on the basis of machinery imports and taking into account some budget variables of joint-stock companies, can be summarized as follows. The textile sector, stimulated by expectations created by the 1887 tariff and not very dependent on bank credit, invested heavily during the 1890s. Finance came mostly from retained profits but also, in the period 1888–91, from new capital issues on the stock market. The large firms in the engineering and metal-making sectors were, instead, hit both by the reduction in bank credit and by the sharp fall in their own profits, forcing them to productive and financial reorganization, an excellent example of which is that of Terni.[11] Finally, there was the case of the growing electrical industry whose investments depended mainly on the possibility of placing their shares on the stock market. The upward movement of share prices between 1888 and 1891 allowed firms to finance themselves through capital issues. The successive fall in share prices made it almost impossible to resort to the market until 1896 when, among other things, the placement of new issues was made easier as a result of the appearance of financial intermediaries such as the so-called 'German banks'.[12]

The collapse of the banking system

The withdrawal of foreign capital after 1887 was in part compensated for by selling abroad large quantities of state bonds (600 million in three fiscal years). An indication of the precariousness of the Italian position in foreign markets can be seen in the fact that a considerable part of foreign debt had to take the form of 10 and 12 month Treasury Bills. The tension on the international capital markets – the so-called Baring crisis in London and the failure of the *Comptoire d'Escompte* in Paris – coincided with the new difficulties of the Turin banks, which were stemmed only temporarily by the above mentioned 1887 interventions by the banks of issue. A new and more serious confidence crisis hit the Italian banking system. This went hand-in-hand with the effects of a further worsening of the cycle in real variables and prices which took place both in Italy and the rest of Europe from the end of 1890 onwards.

The situation soon became very serious for the whole banking system and in particular for the two leading credit banks and some of the banks of issue. In 1887 both the Credito Mobiliare and the Banca Generale found themselves burdened with illiquid assets as much because of finance granted to large metal-making and engineering firms as because of the cover offered to the Banca Tiberina, the Società dell'Esquilino, and the Banco Sconto e Sete which were in serious difficulty because of excess credit granted to building speculation. The credit of last resort interventions of that year gave the impression that the leading banks 'had once again found their ancient solidity and security.'[13]

But the losses were to continue. Those of Credito Mobiliare totalled 30 million between 1887 and 1891. The Banca Generale was hit by the difficulties of the Esquilino, by the collaspe of the Banca di Milano, by the fall in property value in Naples, and by the very poor performance of the building firms and railways, in which it had invested heavily.[14]

At the same time the Banca Nazionale del Regno, the Banco di Napoli, the Banca Romana and the Banca Nazionale Toscana found themselves with undesirably illiquid portfolios. The government, in inviting these banks of issue to re-finance illiquid banks such as the Tiberina, authorized an increase in currency in circulation: the liquidity thus created was used to re-discount very low quality bills. In August 1889, the Tiberina, Esquilino and Sconto e Sete were in such precarious conditions owing to finance granted to construction that 'they would have failed had they not been saved by a massive intervention by the banks of issue. In order to save them the government intervened, authorizing the issue of banknotes to a value of 50 million lire in excess [of the legal limit], without even minimum reserve ratios.'[15] It has been suggested that these frequent increases of currency in circulation facilitated the abuses which were by then being whispered of in circles close to the government and the banking world.[16] The rumours originated in the fact that an inspection of the banks of issue ordered in 1889 by the Minister of Agriculture, Trade and Industry, who had supervisory power, and led by Senator Alvisi and by a Treasury official (Biagini) was kept secret so as to avoid damaging confidence in the banking system – already quite shaken by the difficulties of so many institutes. In these circumstances, however, secrecy, when it is not absolute is a worse expedient than frank information. As would be revealed later, the Alvisi–Biagini enquiry discovered serious irregularities in the management of the Banca Romana by its governor Tanlongo: an excess of currency in circulation above the legal limit and even the clandestine printing of banknotes with already existing serial numbers to a value of 9 million lire. These irregularities had been made possible by the easy-going ways and unscrupulousness of those in charge at the Banca Romana but had their origin in the bank's overall situation of illiquidity due to the lending policy adopted in previous years. In 1892–3 the events in the former bank of the Papal States were closely intertwined not only with a ruthless political struggle between Crispi and Giolitti, but also with the project of reforming the banks of issue. It must be stressed that the serious losses and illiquid assets were not limited to the leading commercial banks, but also involved the banks of issue. The number of unpaid bills was growing; reaching, in 1891, almost 10 per cent of the total.[17]

The crisis came to a head with the winding-up of the two leading

Italian banks, closely linked to so many economic events in the first thirty years after Unification. After 1891 the Credito Mobiliare tried to convert into a bank for short-term commercial credit along the lines of the Credit Lyonnais. The 1891 operating results were encouraging enough to lead to a new capital issue. However, the costs involved in the change-over to deposit bank, with a large increase in the number of branches throughout the country, were too high for a structure weakened by the losses of the previous three years. In November 1893 the Credito Mobiliare had to request a moratorium. In May 1894 the bank ceased trading.

A similar fate was reserved for the Banca Generale, also heavily tied up. In 1892 and 1893 the prices of its shares fell sharply. The resulting lack of public confidence in the bank led to a rush on deposits, which by the end of 1893 had become a landslide. The Banca Generale went into liquidation in January 1894.

The failure of the two leading Italian banks was accompanied by that of numerous minor intermediaries, the liquidation of the Banca Romana and the reorganization of the banks of issue.

Crisis and reorganization of the banks of issue

The crisis of 1893 did not only involve the two main commercial banks and a good number of medium-sized ones, but also struck at the heart of the system: the banks of issue. The problem of reforming the banking law regulating the latter became crucial. This problem had been largely ignored by governments and public opinion since the debates preceding the 1874 Banking Act. Various reform projects received little attention until 1891 when the two Tuscan banks and the Banca Nazionale reached a merger agreement. This merger, inspired by Crispi, was shelved when his second government fell and the Rudinì government was formed. In 1892 the two Tuscan banks agreed to merge,[18] but nothing was done owing to opposition from the then Treasury Minister, Luzzatti.

The banking situation was precarious in the extreme when Giolitti came to power (5 May 1892). The Prime Minister, certainly close enough to the Banca Romana to make Tanlongo senator on the eve of the November 1892 elections, preferred to wait for an overall reform before proposing new mergers. Strengthened by his electoral victory, he presented a bill (December 1892) for the extension of the privilege of issue to the existing banks for another six years. However, the reaction from various quarters, including those nearest to the banks of issue, which felt the need for more radical measures better suited to facing the deterioration in their own position, led Giolitti to withdraw his plan.

On 20 December 1892, after much hesitation, two Members of Parliament, Colajanni and Gavazzi, revealed to the Chamber the results of the 1889 inquiry on the banks of issue and, in particular, the serious irregularities of the Banca Romana. An administrative inquiry immediately ordered by the government and approved by the Chamber soon discovered in this institute 'the existence of illegally-issued notes to the tune of 65 million lire (which almost doubled the currency in circulation allowed to the Bank) and a 20 million lire cash deficit, badly hidden by fictitious operations, and they discovered, furthermore, that in 1891 duplicates of banknotes already in circulation had been printed to a value of about 40 million lire[19] and that balance sheets had been falsified for the previous twenty years. Following the inquiry, Tanlongo and the Chief Cashier Lazzaroni were arrested along with others involved. There was also the mysterious death of a Member of Parliament shortly before he was due to be arrested.

The whole affair amounted to a major scandal, shaking the confidence of the banks of issue. Giolitti took up again his old plans for the merger of the banks of issue; the two Tuscan banks and the Banca Nazionale, in merging, would have to take on the liquidation of the Banca Romana. An agreement to this effect was signed on 18 January 1893 and was approved in February by the general meetings of the three institutes. In his speech of 27 February to the shareholders of the Banca Nazionale, the Chairman, Grillo, returned to the old idea of a single bank of issue. More bitterly, a few days earlier, he had not hidden the fact that he had 'always longed for other beginnings for the Banca d'Italia.'[20]

In the following months the government prepared a bill on this subject. Without going into the details of the various phases of discussion, tied to the political repercussions of the Banca Romana scandal, it is important to recall the terms of the matter. In synthesis, these could be found in the implicit contradiction of the fact that the banks of issue, which were assigned highly delicate tasks of public importance, remained private companies whose shareholders were mainly if not solely interested in maximizing profits and the resulting dividends. The privilege of issuing legal tender was granted to a limited number of banks and was governed by precise regulations. In return for this privilege, the banks of issue paid a tax to the Treasury. In many circumstances, the state asked the banks, in particular the Nazionale, to carry out tasks not provided for by the existing laws: such was the case of the 1866 loan. Faced with similar requests, the Bank reacted typically by trying to reach terms of agreement that would satisfy both the Treasury, on which its very existence depended, and its shareholders. In 1866, in return for the loan, the Nazionale obtained the suspension of the obligation to convert its own banknotes into gold on demand. In 1893 the state asked the banks of issue to absorb the currency in circulation of the Banca Romana: prejudice against the lira itself would have been great if, as a consequence of the liquidation of the former bank of the Papal States, its banknotes had fallen sharply in value. Owing to this intervention in the public interest, the Nazionale and the two Tuscan banks had to budget considerable costs for the acquisition of the unpaid bills of the Banca Romana. The shareholders were obviously reluctant to take on such costs and asked the Treasury for compensation. However, the political climate and public opinion were not favourable to the banks of issue involved in numerous irregularities, if not in outright scandals, and which had undertaken operations of dubious economic worth. The negotiations in the early months of 1893 were complex: the Treasury wanted a complete reform of the circulation and issue system; the banks, although having the same interests at heart, were concerned primarily with protecting their own profits. The situation was further complicated by the involvement of some important politicians in the running of the Banca Romana and by the use for personal and party struggle to which the whole question of issue reform was subject. The bill – mainly Giolitti's personal work, it seems – was presented to the Chamber in March and was discussed by a special committee under Boselli's chairmanship. After a heated debate and lengthy negotiations the new Banking Act was finally passed on 10 August 1893.

The new law made provision for the creation on 1 January 1894 of the Banca d'Italia – fruit of the merger of the Banca Nazionale del Regno, the Banca Nazionale Toscana and the Banca Toscana di Credito – with the considerable capital of 300 million lire. Seventy-three per cent of the 1,097 million fixed as the ceiling of currency in circulation was assigned to the new institute, 22 per cent to the Banco di Napoli, and the remaining 5 per cent to the Banco di Sicilia. State loans were excluded from the limit. Banknotes were convertible and a metal reserve requirement equal to 40 per cent of currency in circulation was established. A reduction in circulation to only 864 million over ten years was also provided for. Furthermore the law laid down precise rules as to the operations permitted to the banks of issue, which were to limit themselves strictly to discounting bills with maturities not exceeding four months and loans not exceeding six months.

The Banca d'Italia took on the liquidation of the Banca Romana and committed itself to replacing the latter's banknotes with its own and to liquidating its liabilities over twenty years.

In the second part of 1893 the financial situation deteriorated dramatically. The flight of capital produced a depreciation of the exchange rate; gold payments were again suspended. Hoarding by the public led to the disappearance from circulation of small metal coins and to the circulation of dubious private promissory notes.

While the crisis of the Credito Mobiliare and the Banca Generale was coming to a close, the confidence of international markets towards Italy was diminishing rapidly, producing a fall in the price of Italian securities in the European stock markets. In the meantime, the trial of those responsible for the fraudulent bankruptcy of the Banca Romana ended with their acquittal. Popular uprisings increased in violence, especially in Sicily.

On 23 November a commission of seven Members of Parliament nominated to cast light on the political responsibilities of the Banca Romana affair presented their findings to the Chamber. The accusation against Giolitti – that of having received monies from the Bank – was declared not proven. However, the Prime Minister was censured for his trust in Tanlongo, by now a bankrupt, and for his silence in Parliament on the Alvisi–Biagini inquiry. The day after, the first Giolitti cabinet resigned at a moment of extreme economic and social crisis during which the struggle for power was conducted on the battlefield of the real or presumed 'scandals' which made a tremendous impression on public opinion and which at the same time struck at the roots of domestic and international confidence in the leading financial institutions of the country. It is likely that a firm and discreet intervention would have avoided the consequences for the country of the failure of the Mobiliare and the Generale. Such intervention did not take place owing both to a lack of clear vision and to the widespread idea that it was dangerous to increase circulation. Moreover, in these months none of the factions fighting for power had sufficient authority, moral or otherwise, to act effectively, and each thought only of getting the maximum political advantage from the situation.

In the new government, led by Crispi, the Ministries of Finance and Treasury were given to Sonnino who had been one of the opposers of the Bank Act, which he had seen as an inadequate compromise solution for the situation which, in his view, should have required the creation of a single monopolistic bank of issue. According to Sonnino, it was only in that way, and by increasing the personal responsibility of the directors of the new bank in safeguarding the regulations relating to currency circulation, that the undesirable growth of the latter could have been contained.

As so often happens the measures hoped for when in opposition turned out to be unfeasible, given the complexity of the problems the government had to deal with: on 23 January Sonnino had hurriedly to authorize the increase in circulation above the limits fixed in August, which had been operative for a mere twenty-three days. This was due to a run on deposits produced by the crisis in the Mobiliare and the Generale.[21] One month later (21 February) a new law authorized a large issue of non-convertible notes and gave power to the Bank of Italy and the southern banks to convert, at will, their own banknotes into metal or notes issued by the state. For the second time, Italy went off the gold standard. Although the situation was to improve considerably in the following decade and the 'premium' would disappear altogether, Italy would officially return to gold convertibility only in December 1927.

The Act of 21 February laid down that the state must give 200 million of its own notes to the three banks of issue 'as replacement for an equal sum in gold which the banks themselves would have to make available to the state Treasury.'[22] The rationale of the measure consisted in not allowing the banks of issue to take advantage of inconvertibility. On this point there was a harsh confrontation between the Treasury Minister and the Banca d'Italia whose Governor, Grillo, resigned in protest.[23] His successor, Marchiori, probably Sonnino's own choice, had to undertake in the following months the difficult task of mediating between the Ministry and the shareholders of the Bank. This was an important landmark on the path towards the creation of a modern central bank. On this occasion, 'the two concepts of those who considered the Bank as the property of the shareholders and of those who qualified it as an organ of the state' were explicitly faced.[24] Although other questions came into play, the conflict was actually about what role to give the Bank of Italy.

The healing of the breach between shareholders and government was inevitable when the former, even when faced with the drop in securities prices, realized that their Bank could not prosper in continuous conflict with the Treasury, and when the latter saw that it could not reform the financial system of the country without counting on the unconditional support of the Banca d'Italia. Negotiations took place which ended on 30 October with the signing of an agreement by which the Bank of Italy assumed at its own risk the liquidation of the Banca Romana obtaining in return the monopoly as State Treasurer. If the interests of shareholders were safeguarded, Sonnino was right in claiming 'to have procured great benefit for the state'[25] and the premises were laid down for giving the Bank of Italy an even more central role in the financial system of the country. Such a role, deriving in part from the State Treasury monopoly, could not be arrived at fully before the legacy of the Banca Romana had been eliminated. A strategy along these lines was immediately imposed. The fact that at the end of this episode the 'public' role of the Banca d'Italia was established, found confirmation in the awareness of this fact among its directors. Marchiori, General Manager of the Banca d'Italia, was fully aware of its new public role when summarizing the history of the agreement to the Board, stated that the Bank 'could not . . . as a private institution, sit back and wait for its own future; as the main element in the national economy, its problems became problems which went well beyond the sphere of particular interest.'[26]

Chapter ten

The 'Age of Giolitti'

The *belle époque* of the world economy

The period that Italian historians often refer to as 'the Age of Giolitti' coincided with a spell of exceptional prosperity for the world economy. An acceleration of production, especially in manufacturing, was accompanied by a more than proportional expansion in international trade and in movements of capital and labour, in a context of a slight increase in prices and of stability in exchange rates. This period is generally seen as the *'belle époque'* of bourgeois society; it appears especially fortunate if seen in the light of the instability of the 1920s, and of the mass unemployment which characterized most of the following decade. 'What an extraordinary episode in the economic progress of man − Keynes wrote in 1919 − that age which came to an end in August 1914.'[1]

Among the factors characterizing this 'golden age' of world capitalism, scholars have included a 'second industrial revolution' which saw developments in the productive use of electricity; the spread of the internal combustion engine and several other innovations particularly in industrial chemistry, appearing, as Schumpeter would say, 'swarmlike' to generate a long wave of expansion. The discovery of new mineral deposits; the use of refrigerator ships to import fresh meat from the Australian and Argentine prairies; the mining of new gold in Russia and the Transvaal, would all contribute to a better exploitation of each country's comparative advantages and, therefore, to a tremendous increase in international movements of goods and of factors of production. When all this came to an abrupt halt at the outbreak of the First World War, the damage was such that many considered it irreparable.

The years between Crispi's resignation (1896) and the assassination of Archduke Ferdinand (1914) were characterized, in Italy, by a growth in gross domestic product which, according to the available statistics, was for the first time much higher than that in

Table 10.1 Average annual growth of GDP, population and per capita product 1896–1913

Country	GDP	Population	Per capita GDP
Australia	3.2	1.9	2.1
Austria*	2.5	1.0	1.3
Belgium	2.0	1.0	1.5
Canada	4.4	2.4	2.0
Denmark	3.4	1.2	2.0
France	1.9	0.2	2.0
Germany	3.2	1.4	1.8
Japan	2.8	1.2	1.6
Italy	2.8	0.7	2.1
Norway	2.7	0.9	1.8
United Kingdom	1.7	0.8	0.9
United States	4.3	1.9	2.4
Sweden	3.2	0.8	2.4

Source: Estimates from A. Maddison, Phases of Capitalist Development, Oxford: Oxford University Press, 1982.

Note: * 1919 borders.

population and therefore considerably increased the amount of goods and services available to the average citizen. The change relative to the previous thirty-year period was such that most historians would place Italy's 'take-off' during the 'Giolittian era'. Indeed many of the characteristics of Kuznets' modern economic growth took shape in those twenty years.

Table 10.1 compares the average annual growth rates of GDP, population and per capita output in thirteen countries. With few exceptions, the spread around the average growth rate of per capita income was small: nine countries fall into the 1.8–2.4 per cent interval. Compared with that of other countries, Italy's growth appears remarkable, mainly thanks to the limited demographic increase which was due in part to massive emigration. It was during these years that Italy, or rather north Italy, began to 'catch up' with those Continental countries which had left her behind in agricultural production, trade, and manufacturing. Ninety years later, at the time of writing, despite the standstill and contradictions relating both to productive structure and to great social problems, this 'catching up' seems to be almost completed since per capita GDP, measured at market exchange rates, is more or less the same in Italy as in the United Kingdom.

Macroeconomics

The year 1896 conveniently marks the turning point both in the political and in the economic sphere since it saw the end of Crispi's imperialistic and authoritarian dreams. Convenient though this may be, the year itself does not appear particularly significant as far as the cyclical behaviour of the main variables is concerned. If one looks at the estimates of industrial production, the trough of the cycle was in 1892, according to the indices of Gerschenkron and Fenoaltea, or 1893 according to ISTAT. The depression in investments lasted much longer. Fenoaltea's recent series for investment in building and construction[2] shows it falling by almost 30 per cent between 1894 and 1889 and only in 1902–3 again reaching the level of ten years before. Another partial indicator, the apparent consumption in industrial machinery, calculated by Warglien,[3] is characterized by shorter cycles, with low points in 1892 and 1897, but remains steady, at a relatively low level, between 1895 and 1898. The ISTAT series for investments in machinery and transport equipment also gives 1898 as the lowest point since 1881.

These time sequences not only confirm that fluctuations in production levels were slighter than those in investments, but also tend to rule out that the latter acted as 'motor' of the economic revival in the second half of the 1890s. The stability of public and private consumption throughout the crisis mitigated the effects of fluctuations in investment on aggregate demand. The slow but steady revival in consumption from 1894 on suggests that the initially slow reversion of the cycle was determined principally by the behaviour of this variable. Overseas demand, too, seems to have contributed considerably to production revival: between 1891 and 1898 Italian exports increased at an average annual rate of 5 per cent.

The acceleration in development towards the end of the century and the subsequent rapid growth lasting until 1907, when it slowed down once more, can be seen in Table 10.2. The period was characterized by increased rates of investment both in machinery and in private and public construction; by a strong increase in manufacturing output, and by a respectable development in agricultural production. On the contrary, the growth of exports was relatively low while imports grew much faster, producing significant deficits in the foreign trade balance.

Towards the end of the century the change in expectations was reflected in a new wave of investments which took place in a very favourable environment. The supply of financial capital and of labour were both highly elastic; and import requirements (particularly for machinery and raw materials) could easily be met thanks

Table 10.2 Growth rates of GDP, industrial production, investments, and exports 1894–1913

Period	GDP	Investments		Industrial production			Exports
		Total	In public works and construction				
	(1)	(2)	(3)	(4)	(5)	(6)	(7)
1894–9	1.3	4.7	−4.0	1.9	5.0	5.0	3.9
1899–1907	3.4	13.9	9.3	5.9	6.5	7.1	3.5
1907–13	1.8	0.9	8.3	2.0	3.2	4.1	2.0

Sources: ISTAT columns (1) (2) (4) (7): P. Ercolani, 'Documentazione statistica di base', in G. Fuà (ed.) Lo sviluppo economico in Italia, Milan: Angeli, 1969; column (3): S. Fenoaltea, 'Edilizia e opere pubbliche in Italia', in Rivista di Storia Economica, (IV), 1987; column (5): A. Gerschenkron, Economic Backwardness in Historical Perspective, Cambridge (Mass.): Belknap Press, 1962; column (6): S. Fenoaltea, 'Italy', in P.K. O'Brien (ed.) Railways and the Economic Development of Western Europe 1830–1914, London: Macmillan, 1983.

to the rapid growth in earnings from tourism and, most noticeably, from emigrants' remittances. The change in the balance of political power in favour of those forces most aware of the needs of production requirements; the reorganization of the banking system in 1894–5; and, above all, the revival in demand and production in the major European countries and in the Americas created a climate of stability and optimism, which, from 1898 on, was reflected in the demand for investment beginning from that of long-delayed replacements. This demand found no obstacles either in the supply of finance capital or that of physical capital. As far as the first is concerned, the fall in interest rates does not appear as important as does the end of credit rationing in the early 1890s, the 'crowding-in' deriving from budget surpluses, and, mainly for medium-size firms, the increasing capacity for self-financing. The latter derives from a probable shift in income distribution in favour of profits implicit in a growth model 'à la Lewis' which seems to fit pretty well Italy's conditions in those years. Taking Fuà's conservative estimates, output per worker increased at least at an average annual rate of 2.9 per cent between 1897 and 1907.[4] The growth in real wages is estimated by Zamagni[5] to be around 2.2 per cent. Considering that the terms of trade moved in favour of manufacturing one may argue that there is some empirical support for an interpretation à la Lewis of Italy's development in the Giolittian era. The fact that industrial investments grew more rapidly than production would confirm this interpretation.

As is often the case in relatively backward countries poorly endowed with raw materials, the growth of the 'modern' sector led to a more than proportional increase in imports. The balance of trade surpluses which characterized the slump of the 1890s[6] turned into deficits during the following decade: in 1908 currency revenue from exports covered only 79 per cent of import outlays. Trade deficits of this size continued until the First World War. Despite this, exchange rates remained extraordinarily stable: in many years the paper lira was exchanged at a premium relative to its official gold parity, thanks to the fact that, despite the unfavourable balance of trade, the balance of payments on current account often showed large surpluses until 1907. The '*belle époque*' created a new demand for tourism in the more advanced countries, which Italy was particularly able to satisfy. However, it was principally the great transoceanic migration that generated a strong inflow of remittances in foreign currency. As in the boom of 1950–63, the earnings from these two 'invisible exports' allowed industrial growth to be free from external constraints. Less clear is the role played by long-term capital movements: what little is known about them, however, is enough to allow us to rule out their having played, at aggregate level, a quantitatively important role. Foreign direct investment in individual industries, however, was a vehicle for the transfer of technology and entrepreneurial skills with considerable effects on productivity and long-term growth.

The 1907–8 crisis interrupted development in the 'Age of Giolitti': there followed – according to all available estimates – a fall in growth rates of production. The rate of growth for GDP was halved and supported by public consumption (which increased by 6.9 per cent a year between 1907 and 1913 as against a mere 1.5 per cent in private consumption). The thrust deriving from exports also diminished. The role played by investments after the 1907–8 crisis is less clear. The growth rate of the ISTAT series (see Table 10.2) is biased by the fact that 1907 was a year of high investments: average investments in the period 1908–13 exceeded by about 10 per cent those of the previous six years. Fenoaltea's estimates on the construction industry indicate very dynamic investment behaviour in this sector.

Transformations and development of agriculture

Bolton King has estimated the average value of Italian agricultural production for the three years following Crispi's resignation at about 4 billion current lire.[7] O'Brien and Toniolo have estimated the same production for the years 1909–11 at 8.3 billion lire.[8] Allowing for price increases, one would still have an annual rate of growth in gross product of agriculture of about 5 per cent in real terms between the second Rudinì government and the war in Libya. In fact, it is likely that Bolton King underestimated the product of Italian agriculture at the end of the century.[9] According to the Fuà estimates, the real rate of growth over the above-mentioned periods was about 2 per cent per annum: an estimate likely to be not too far off the mark. Even accepting the most conservative estimates, there is little doubt that a radical change in trend took place relative to the previous thirty years. Given the specific problems of agricultural statistics during those years it is difficult to give an exact date for the beginning of the acceleration of the trend. The Fuà estimates, however, seem to indicate an almost stationary trend during Crispi's premiership so that it seems that agricultural production speeded up only in the last years of the century, together with industrial production. The synchrony of this long phase of expansion in the two sectors must be underlined as it constitutes one of the elements to be taken into account for an overall interpretation of the nature and causes of modern economic growth in Italy.

The growth in production of the main agricultural products during the 'Age of Giolitti' is summarized in Table 10.3 in which the base for the indices is the five-year period in the 1880s which preceded the introduction of the customs tariff and the trade war with France.

Table 10.3 Agricultural production by sectors 1895–1913 (1884–8 = 100)

Sectors	1895–9	1901–5	1909–13
Cereals	100	133	137
Legumes	106	137	148
Potatoes, vegetables, industrial crops	129	170	245
Fruit and citrus fruit	94	126	151
Olive tree products	79	104	69
Vine products	92	118	147
Zootechnical products	112	117	132
Total	103	124	139

Source: P. Ercolani, 'Documentazione statistica di base', in G. Fuà (ed.) *Lo sviluppo economico in Italia*, Milan: Angeli, 1969, vol. III, p. 410.

On the demand side, traditionally, the first three and the last sectors produce mainly for the home markets while the others also work for overseas trade.

Production of cereals, which accounted for about 20 per cent of total agricultural output, was sustained by high import duties during this period. The duty on wheat was raised from 1.3 to 3 lire per quintal in 1887, to 5 lire the following year and to 7.5 lire in 1894.[10] This level, which remained unchanged until the First World War, apart from a slight reduction in 1898, guaranteed protection equal to 33 to 38 per cent of the average import price, not very different from that prevailing across the Alps.[11] Customs duties allowed producers to compete with American grains which had become highly competitive in the second half of the 1880s. The trend in demand for domestic cereals clearly depended on the terms of trade taking duty into account, and on domestic consumption. The latter rose from 41.7 to 62.0 million quintals between 1890–4 and 1909–13, with an average annual growth rate of 2 per cent. About 20 per cent of pre-war domestic demand for cereals (excluding rice) was met by imports.[12]

Domestic demand explains most of the strong growth in the production of legumes, potatoes, vegetables, and materials for industrial use. The spread of sugarbeet cultivation, also supported by customs duties,[13] led to drop in sugar imports which fell from an average of 751,000 quintals in the last decade of the century to a mere 93,000 quintals in that immediately preceding Italy's entry into the First World War.

Exports, particularly of wine, were indirectly favoured by the ending, in 1898, of the customs war with France. This war had been sparked off by the 1887 tariff which had exacerbated the political tension already existing between the two countries. After 1900, however, exports of vine products dropped considerably and the growing production was absorbed by the home market where, for the first time, the income of part of the working masses rose above mere subsistence level.

Supply did not adjust immediately to the demand dynamics produced by the rise in urban and industrial incomes; all the same it showed surprising elasticity, an indication that the Italian agricultural world, far from being static, was able to respond to market signals. Agricultural policy was aimed at stimulating 'the growth in productivity and technical progress.'[14] The latter, however, took place mainly in the Po valley: thus increasing economic dualism between the north and south of the country.

The pillars of agricultural policy were customs duties, agrarian credit, technical assistance, vocational education, and land reclamation. These were not new approaches since the more farsighted members of the agricultural bourgeoisie had already moved along these lines, at least from the times of the Jacini inquiry onwards, but the revival in demand and accumulation after a long rural crisis widened the prospects for success to state action in this area. Moreover, larger financial resources were allocated for this purpose during the Giolittian era.

Customs policy did not consist – either in this or in other sectors – in the revision of the 1887 Tariff Act, but rather in the use of its harshness to negotiate new trade treaties in order to obtain better conditions for Italian exporters without giving up what was to remain, until the First World War, one of the mainstays of the tariff structure in almost all the European countries: the duty on grain.

The first Agrarian Credit Act, passed in 1887, remained viturally inoperative, mainly because of the slow responsiveness of the credit institutions in issuing the special bonds necessary to finance agrarian credit. From 1897 on *ad hoc* institutes sprang up in many parts of the country, drawing a large share of their liabilities directly from the Treasury.

Agricultural education developed in this period. In particular one should remember the flourishing 'peripatetic chairs', so called because they changed location every few years. Between 1886 (when the first of these institutions was founded in Rovigo) and 1897 the 'chairs' were created and maintained by local authorities; later they received considerable help from the state and were given the same legal status as experimental institutes and university-level courses.

These years also saw a turning point in the field of land reclamation. Until then 'reclamation had come across many obstacles. The main one was that relating to the allocation of the contingent expenditure between the state and private citizens. The "Baccarini law" of 1882 had made an important step forward in clarifying matters by dividing works into two categories and recognizing state competence'[15] where the public interest was considerable due to the presence of malaria. This law, however, remained mainly inoperative. This was due both to the agricultural depression and the limited resources available for land reclamation:[16] expectations that the programme would fail often prevented its getting off the ground. An Act of 1893, amended in 1902, made provisions for the creation and financing of the land reclamation consortia among farmers. In 1903, coercive measures were taken for the reclamation of the Agro Romano which paved the way for three laws in 1911 which crowned 'the intense reclamation activity throughout the country during the previous decade introducing for the first time the concept of complete reclamation and empowering the state to provide for compulsory cultivation on reclaimed lands.'[17] A ministerial report in 1905 specified that about 768,000 hectares had already been reclaimed and that work was being done on a further

400,000; it also noted the greater speed with which the process had been carried out in nothern Italy, where private landowners had acted as state concessionaries.

In order to understand better the overall reawakening of productive forces in agriculture and the greater attention given to this sector during the Age of Giolitti it is necessary to remember both the tensions and the likely social dynamics present in rural areas at the time. As to the former, one need only recall that the movement of the Sicilian Fasci assumed, from the early 1890s onwards, tones of open revolt which Crispi, who had just returned to power, dealt with harshly. In 1897, both in rural areas and in many cities there were demonstrations and riots against the high price of bread, which led the Rudinì government to lower the duty on wheat from 7.5 to 5.0 lire per quintal between January and July 1898. This measure turned out to be inadequate and tension rose throughout the country during the spring of 1898. In May, the uprisings were brought to a bloody halt by the cannons of General Bava Beccaris in Milan and by the harsh repression in the rest of the country. The situation gave cause for thought on the part of those who were soon to form a political majority under the leadership of Giolitti. They thought it advisable to assume a more open attitude towards both the cause of the tension and the problem of political representation of the popular forces in the Socialist Party, founded in 1892, and in the Catholic movement. The agricultural policy mentioned above certainly contributed to the growth of income and accumulation in the sector even if its effects were visible mainly in the north where environmental conditions as much as cultural traditions allowed positive reaction to the stimuli coming from the tariffs, subsidized credit, and reclamation. The rapid strengthening of the Socialist Party, as well as of the Catholic organizations which had matured with the Opera dei Congressi and the Papal Encylcical *Rerum Novarum*, were expressions of a new social climate in which productive initiatives, such as co-operatives, began to flourish.

The 'big spurt' of industry

In the first chapter it was highlighted not only how the years following Crispi's resignation actually saw the rise, at least from a quantitative point of view, of modern economic growth in Italy, but also how this growth, certainly supported by a considerable increase in agricultural production, was characterized by such exceptional expansion in manufacturing that some would put Italy's 'industrial revolution' in this period.[18] The quantitative appraisal of Italian manufacturing (see Chapter one) relates both to the aggregate rate of growth, with the great differences between the ISTAT estimates and those of Fenoaltea, and to the trend in the leading sectors. As to the latter, it is important to recall the strong dynamics in production of investment and intermediate goods especially in the electrical, steel, engineering, and chemical industries. On the demand side, their growth depended on the rapid increase in that for investment. Supply side conditions were equally important: a 'second European industrial revolution' was under way with the appearance, towards the end of the nineteenth century, of important innovations in the fields of application of electricity to productive processes (electromechanics, electro-chemistry) and in transportation (internal combustion engine). These innovations spread slowly at first, and it was only at the beginning of the new century that they acquired enough quantitative importance to have an impact on entire productive sectors, generate considerable decreases in costs, activate demand from other sectors through forward and backward linkages.

The electrical industry appeared in Italy during the 1880s: the Edison firm was founded in 1882 by a group of engineers and financiers led by Giuseppe Colombo. However, the important developments took place at the beginning of the twentieth century with large hydroelectric projects in the Alps and in the pre-alpine areas. The progress at the same time in techniques for the transportation of electrical energy (particularly in the cable industry, in which Pirelli became one of the most avant-garde world producers) allowed a rapid spread of this type of energy both for industrial and private use. Between 1900 and 1914 Italian production of electricity multiplied sixteen-fold and on the eve of the First World War was at the same level as in France and reached 73 per cent of British output, but only a quarter of that in Germany.

In the manufacturing sector the highest rates of growth were those of the engineering, chemical, and rubber industries. The first was characterized by a dualistic structure in which, alongside the few large firms, there were a variety of flourishing small and tiny productive units, often tied to traditional techniques. In some sectors where Italy had long been dependent on imports (for example, locomotives), these were replaced almost entirely by domestic goods. There was also a first, timid development of exports. Firms such as Breda and Ansaldo were in the forefront of this process. The rapid growth of the machine-tool and industrial machinery sectors was not able to match the exceptional demand deriving from the investment boom and imports of such products increased at least until 1907–8. The automobile industry, destined to be one of the pillars of the Italian manufacturing system, took its first steps during the Age of Giolitti. FIAT began operations in 1899 and Alfa in 1910. However, it was only with the First World War that mass production paved the way for developments in the 1920s and 1930s. As far as the electromechanical industry is concerned, Italy remained dependent on imports from Germany and it was only from 1907–8 on that Italian firms, some of which had been founded with foreign capital, acquired an important share of the domestic market.

According to both the free-traders of the time and to most of today's historians, the potential of the engineering industry was in part sacrificed to the protection given to the steel industry by the 1887 tariff.[19] It is held that the duty on important inputs such as iron and steel increased production costs for the engineering industry relative to their foreign competitors, thus preventing the development of exports. In theory, it is difficult to deny that the protection given to the steel industry made Italian engineering products less competitive, *ceteris paribus*, until 1903 when duty-free imports of iron and steel were allowed for manufacturers destined for export. It must be pointed out, however, that in terms of 'effective protection' the damage done to Italian engineering does not appear quantitatively significant. In fact, exports after 1903 did not increase as one would have expected had the duty on steel really limited the industry's ability to export. At the same time, while 'effective protection' remained positive, domestic production did not meet the increase in domestic demand. These two elements lead one to look beyond the tariff for the causes of the alleged unsatisfactory development of the engineering industry during the Age of Giolitti: one has to take into account the technological gap accumulated so far, the limited size of plants, and the scarcity of managerial talent. Given the circumstances, however, and the high growth rate of the engineering industry, it is difficult to speak of overall failure.

The chemical industry, another future mainstay of Italian growth, developed without state support. Production of sulphuric acid grew by 10.6 per cent a year between 1896 and 1913. Montecatini, until then a mining firm, assumed the lead of the sector, thanks to the business acumen of Guido Donegani. Import substitution was very rapid. In the rubber industry, the Italians were able to compete with the most advanced European producers gaining important orders for undersea cables and developing techniques which allowed the distribution of electricity to places far away from its production site. Pirelli with its direct investments in Spain and other countries, became the first important Italian multinational company.

These were mainly new industries with considerable potential for an increasing productivity through the introduction of autochthonous or imported technical progress. They were also the sectors on which the economic fortunes of a manufacturing country such as Italy, were to rest in the following decades. While it is right for historians to examine the modern and innovative industries closely, it should not be forgotten that the general index of industrial production was still highly sensitive to the behaviour of 'traditional' sectors, such as textiles and food-processing. In 1896, according to Fuà estimates,[20] the value added by the textile sector alone was three times that of the metal-making, engineering, and chemical sectors taken together. This estimate is likely to be inaccurate, but the size of the phenomena leaves little doubt as to the fact that the development of textile production – which between 1896 and 1906 grew at the respectable annual rate of 5.9 per cent – 'explains' a large part of the manufacturing boom in the Giolitti years. The tariff of 1887 had given not insubstantial protection to the cotton sector which with the silk and wool industries had been one of the main components of the Italian manufacturing industry for many years. Since they could count on a fairly solid basis of retained profits for self-financing, the leading textile manufacturers were only marginally affected by the financial crisis of the early 1890s and the sector was able to continue its long-term expansion thanks to the stability in private consumption between 1888 and 1896.

Data on imports of raw cotton suggest that Italian cotton production grew rapidly until 1907, fell during the following three years and began to rise again slowly until the outbreak of war. It is likely that around 1907 there was a real crisis of over-production due to the high prices set by producers in the home market which was well protected from foreign competition. In this situation the practice of 'dumping' (mainly in exports to eastern Europe and the Near East) was intensified. Despite these overproduction problems, depending in part on the hothouse regime in which the cotton producers had wanted to place themselves, the industry made considerable progress both in techniques (rapid machanization of spindles and looms) and in organization.

It is less easy to establish the size of the growth in production of woollen yarn and cloth since the data on inputs of raw materials are unreliable: around 80 per cent of raw materials were produced at home and the statistics relating to sheep breeding are particularly inaccurate. However, excess investments were avoided and it is likely that the years after 1908 were not as problematic as they were for the cotton industry. Some of the large firms around Biella and Vicenza were reorganized, while in Prato 'there emerged a new type of production based on the recycling of scraps for industrial purposes.'[21]

The silk industry presents a complex and, on the whole, not very positive picture. The main novelty of the period was the appearance of strong competition from Japan, and most of the producers, especially in the spinning sector, were unable to respond to the challenge with the increase in productivity which would have been the only way to reduce production costs. The American crisis of 1907, with the failure of the American Silk Company which made abundant use of Italian imports, hit hard. Moreover, this crisis was followed by a series of bad cocoon harvests so that in 1913 about a third of processed raw material came from abroad. 'The industry which had always been free-tradist now began gradually to ask for state intervention, even if only for compensation along the lines of the protection given to other sectors.'[22] A 1912 law made provision for bonuses, incentives, and easier credit.

Though difficult to quantify, the progress made in the food processing industry was of great importance. According to the Fuà data, production grew by 6.2 per cent a year between 1896 and 1907 and by 2.7 per cent in the following six years. One should also note the large investments in the sugar industry, protected by a sturdy tariff barrier which, however, industrialists never deemed satisfactory.

On the whole, going by the information now available on the levels and flows of production in the various sectors, one is led to conclude that the boom in Italian industrial production was determined both by considerable trend acceleration in traditional final demand oriented sectors, and less affected by the crisis of the previous ten years, and by a boom in value added by the technologically advanced sectors starting out from small or insignificant production levels. The events in the latter group can be read in terms of a real 'discontinuity' of the production index attributable to changes in technology and expectations, which created a particularly long cyclical upswing of investments after the long depression of the early 1890s.

The labour market

According to Vitali's estimates[23] Italy's labour force, about 16 million, grew very little between 1901 and 1911. The ratio of males to females oscillated around 2:1. In the same period the natural increase in population was near to 3.8 million.

In 1901 agriculture still absorbed 59 per cent of the labour force. Living conditions and labour contracts in rural areas varied so much throughout the peninsula that it is impossible to provide an overall, let alone an approximate, view of them. In the early twentieth century most of the southern day-labourers considered themselves lucky if they managed to put together 120–150 working days a year. As to the share-croppers and small owner-farmers in the centre–north, it is only too well known that the size of most of the estates was such as to leave peasants with a lot of free time. O'Brien and Toniolo[24] have calculated that Italian agricultural production in the years 1908–11 could have been obtained using little less than half of the existing labour force had this been fully employed. Indirect confirmation of the fact that the marginal productivity of agricultural labour was close to zero came during the First World War when, despite the conscription of over two million young male peasants, gross agricultural product dropped only slightly and even then this was probably due to other factors. There is no doubt that in the first decade of the century, one of the main problems of the country both at an economic and at a social level came from an excess of population relative to other available resources and not from an inefficient use of the latter.

Italian rural areas were characterized in this, as in other periods, by a large excess supply of labour on which urban areas could draw at a reasonable cost whenever there was the opportunity of increasing production. After 1896 there were many such opportunities in Italy and even more abroad.

The labour force in Italian industry increased by about 500,000 units between 1901–11, while agriculture lost almost 600,000. It should be noted, by the way, that the migration of a family from the countryside to urban areas results in a 'statistical' fall in the labour force to the extent that, for census purposes, women are normally considered as members of the work force in agriculture while at that time they were considered as housewives and, therefore, excluded from the work force, once they had reached the cities.

The availability of an almost unlimited supply of labour allowed industry to contain wage increases. According to recent calculations,[25] average daily wages rose from 1.86 lire in 1901 to 2.67 lire in 1911; allowing for price inflation there was an average annual increase of real wages of 2.5 per cent, lower than that of productivity. This produced a reduction in the unit cost of labour, which, in the absence of a strong fall in the relative prices of the sector, allowed that increase of profits and accumulation already mentioned. An elastic labour supply was therefore an important condition for the rapid growth in industrial production and investments during the Giolitti years.

It has been said that the labour force remained essentially

unvaried between the two censuses of 1901 and 1911, and that the fall in the agricultural labour force was almost wholly compensated for by the increase in that in industry. However, as we have seen, the natural growth of the population, taken over the decade, was about 3.8 million. Given the high participation rate (48 per cent in 1911), demographic growth should therefore have produced an increase of about 1.8 million in the total labour force. That this did not happen depended in part on the fall, between 1901 and 1911, of three percentage points in the participation rate and to a much greater extent on the net balance of emigration.

Emigration from Italy was a relatively contained phenomenon, despite having shown signs of speeding up, until the beginning of the 1890s. The migration rate rose from 0.38 per cent in 1876 to 1.06 per cent in 1900, with a considerable increase in the last decade. In this first phase roughly half of Italian emigrants went to European countries. Among the overseas destinations, Latin America took in almost a third of the total migration flow.[26] Between 1876–80 the vast majority of emigrants came from northern regions (76.5 per cent) and only 12.5 per cent from the south. Twenty years later the provinces of the ex-Kingdom of the Two Sicilies contributed 33 per cent of the total, and the north-east (Veneto and Friuli) 34.4 per cent. In the fifteen years before the First World War, there were considerable quantitative and qualitative changes in the phenomenon. Around 8.8 million people left Italy: that is, about a third of the total expatriation during the entire post-Unification history of Italy to the present day. The migration rate rose from 1 per cent in 1900 to 2.4 per cent in 1913. At the same time, there were significant changes both in the emigrants' destination and their origin. Forty per cent of the Italian workers who left Italy between 1901 and 1915 went to the United States. Brazil became less important; while Argentina saw large seasonal movements of Italian labourers taking advantage of the different harvest times in the two countries. In this period, 45 per cent emigrated from the south and 16.5 per cent from the Veneto and Friuli.[27]

Taking into account the number of returning emigrants, which increased rapidly after 1900, the net migration balance was 1.2 million: not all of these were subtracted from the work force, but along with the reduction in the participation rate, the phenomenon explains the essentially stationary level of the working population between the two censuses. As a rough guide one can say that for every worker who moved from agriculture to domestic industry in this period there were two who left Italy to work in the 'modern' sector abroad. The expansion of the world economy and the increased facility in travelling were important factors in economic growth for at least two reasons. First, given the fact that the country's main problem was that of an excess of population in relation to agricultural resources, so that only a rapid development in the urban industrial sector could ease such pressure and allow the growth of per capita income, the economic dynamics of less populated countries allowed such a process to take place faster than in the absence of such a dynamic international labour market. Second, one should note the importance of emigrants' remittances in a country whose balance of trade, structurally tending towards deficit, was subjected to further tensions owing to the strong demand for imports produced by rapid industrialization. In 1908, the trade deficit was 61 per cent of the total value of exported goods; however, import capacity remained high during this period thanks particularly to emigrants' remittances. Without these there would soon have been tensions on the foreign exchange markets which would ultimately have brought about a fall in imports and, therefore, in investments and in the related technical progress with inevitable effects on the growth of industrial production.

The evolution of the financial intermediation system

The liquidation of the two 'French banks' (the Generale and the Credito Mobiliare) in 1893 deprived the intermediation system of credit institutions which had contributed to mobilizing the financial capital necessary for the construction of the railway network; had supported the growth of investments in the 1880s and had established important links with international finance. The vacuum was filled by German-type banks. The Banca Commerciale Italiana (Comit) was established in October 1894[28] and the Credito Italiano the following February. The initial capital of the former, 20 million lire, was underwritten by banks in Germany (78 per cent), Austria (13 per cent), and Switzerland (9 per cent). Credito Italiano was founded by adding fresh capital, in part German, to that of the Banca di Genova whose business name was modified. To some extent the two new institutes drew on the traditions of the two 'French' banks, absorbing part of their staff and customers.

According to Gerschenkron these two banks, and particularly the Banca Commerciale, played a crucial role in promoting industrial growth during the Age of Giolitti.[29] More recently, Confalonieri has shown that their importance as suppliers of industrial entrepreneurial talent was negligible: these were not, after all, lacking in the country.[30] Only in the electrical industry did the banks seem to have their own development strategy based on the belief that the new sector offered good profit opportunities.

113

The 'mixed banks' of the German type probably participated in the main business affairs of the country, but – with the exception of some sectors and firms – they did not become 'holding banks', at least not until after the First World War.[31] The word 'mixed' gives a good indication of their wide vision of banking business; that is, the desire to deal mainly with large clients whom they could supply with discounts, loans, carry-overs, foreign currency, medium-term credit, and overall assistance in capital issue operations without, however, creating that symbiosis between bank and industry which was to be typical of the 1920s. The new 'German' banks seem to have played a crucial but indirect role in the process of industrialization. The financial expertise of their management and the links with foreign financial circles proved to be an important innovation in the country's intermediation system, at a moment in which its efficiency was an essential prerequisite for growth. Comit and Credito Italiano became the vertex of a system composed, at least in the centre–north, of a large network of co-operative banks, savings banks and small- and medium-sized joint stock banks. At a time when the ratio of savings to national income was increasing, the supply of credit became cheaper and more readily available to medium-sized firms.

The establishment in 1893 of the Bank of Italy was the decisive step for the creation in Italy of a modern central bank. The first few years were not easy, the main concern being that of liquidating the large illiquid assets of the Banca Romana. However, after the nomination of Stringher as General Manager in 1900, the Bank of Italy took upon itself with ever greater resolution the main operative responsibility in the control of money supply and exchange rates, as well as that of being the lender of last resort. This too was a crucial financial innovation of these years: the financial intermediation system became more stable than it had been a decade earlier.

The slowing down in the issues of government bonds, and the growth of investments and profits produced, for the first time in the history of Italy, a considerable increase in the number of shares traded on the stock exchanges and a boom in their prices which began in 1901 and accelerated from 1905 onwards until their collapse in October 1906. The crisis which followed is interesting mainly because the way in which it was dealt with and overcome was the first stability test and the first success of the financial intermediation system created in 1893.

All the leading banks were drawn into forms of overtrading during the final and rapid upward phase of share prices. The Commerciale forgot its traditional, prudent policy of keeping large liquid risk funds and the Società Bancaria Italiana (SBI) found itself, in 1907, in a serious liquidity crisis.

The latter bank, the third largest in the country, had been established in 1899 as the Società Bancaria Milanese, only becoming 'Italiana' in 1904 when it decided to open branches throughout the country[32] and was regarded favourably in many circles for the 'Italianness' of its capital.[33] This bank's difficulties derived in part from the less than brilliant operations of the previous years and in part from its commitment to supporting share prices from the final months of 1906 onwards.[34] A further fall in those prices in September 1907 made its position untenable and led to fears, even among its rival institutes, that it would be forced to suspend payments and thus create a lack of confidence in the entire banking system among the public with a consequent run on deposits. The Bank of Italy which until then had tried to face the situation with a generous supply of liquidity, realized that more direct and precise intervention was necessary. It therefore promoted the creation of a consortium of three large banks – Zaccaria Pisa, Credito Italiano, and Comit – for an intervention in favour of the SBI. An initial credit of 20 million lire was burned up in a few days while discussions were still taking place on the intervention needed in order to prevent too sharp a fall in share prices.

The second line of credit, 40 million lire, was granted at the end of October with the proviso that management of the SBI be put into the hands 'of the backers (i.e. the above-mentioned consortium) who would strike towards a rapid liquidation of assets' so that the Bank of Italy would effectively 'assume . . . a pre-eminent position in the running of the intervention which was to decide the survival of the SBI.'[35] Stringher, whose constant concern, not only on this occasion, was that of avoiding sudden shifts in the 'balance of power' inside the banking system and the creation of monopolistic positions, did his best to avoid the liquidation of the SBI. The latter devalued its capital and successively increased it with the supply of fresh money. Stringher appointed the head of the Turin branch of the Bank of Italy to be its General Manager. By June 1908, all the debts contracted with the members of the consortium were paid off.

This episode has been described in some detail because it is indicative both of the persistent weaknesses and of the progress made by the country's financial intermediation system in little more than a decade. The fact that the new banks had collected part of the managerial staff and know-how of the former institutes to some extent conditioned their behaviour in a situation of speculative fever fairly similar to that in the 1880s. It has been noted that the

'German banks' 'were not equal to their own position and tasks' not only 'because of their imprudent conduct in the finance markets', but also because 'at the first sign of problems they tried to transfer to the banks of issue the burden of industrial finance' and because they had hardly supported 'the action undertaken by the Bank of Italy to impose . . . a credit policy aimed at keeping the specific functions of the bank of issue and of the credit banks separate, though interlinked.'[36]

However, despite the persistent weakness, steps forward had been made: on the one hand, the banks, however reluctantly, ended up by co-operating with the Bank of Italy and, on the other, the 1907 crisis taught them an important lesson which, later on, made them 'much more prudent in their dealings on the stock exchanges.'[37] The great innovation, however, had been in the creation of a central bank. The Bank of Italy was aware of its role as guarantor of stability in the financial system and, indirectly, in the industrial system and the whole growth process, thanks to its privileged relations with the government and with the credit banks as well as with the business community at large. The 1907 crisis was a sort of baptism by fire for the Bank of Italy in a role far more complex than its already important function as the lender of last resort. In this difficult situation the Bank availed itself of its suasion power both with the government and with the credit institutions. Its action was guided by the conscious aim of avoiding a banking crisis and an almost certain crisis in several large manufacturing firms, but it refused 'to finance indiscriminately the pure and simple salvage of stock market speculation which had been responsible for the instability of the Italian securities market.'[38] Even though it acted in close contact with the government and played a decisive role in its orientation – thanks also to the excellent relations that Stringher had with the Treasury Minister, Carcano – the Bank resisted political pressures for indiscriminate financing of steel groups whose financial conduct had been irresponsible. The autonomy which the leading bank of issue was now reinforcing would later turn out to be one of the most important elements of equilibrium in the system.

After 1907–8, the growth of production and investments slowed down. The 'mixed banks' became more careful in evaluating the risks involved in industrial development. If they failed in further stimulating industrial expansion 'they did so because the situation was one of lasting crisis in many sectors and of reluctance on the part of the investor to invest in shares.'[39] This greater prudence and the unsatisfactory trend in the stock exchanges, however, made the financial problems of some industrial firms more acut, in particular those in the steel sector which, in 1911, had to be 'salvaged' – an operation in which the credit banks participated with the support of the banks of issue.

These circumstances revived the debate on the institutions which governed the financial markets and on the problem of industrial credit. Of particular interest, on the first point, was a bill presented by Nitti in 1913 when he was Minister of Agriculture, Trade and Industry, which proposed giving the Ministry itself a supervisory function on the banks' operations with the aim of promoting a higher ratio of capital to deposits. As far as industrial credit is concerned, there were many requests for it to be precisely regulated by law, essentially by creating 'special credit institutes' for industry and social overhead capital. At this time, however, no important legislation was passed on this matter.

The problem of industrial credit became more acute when the Great War was in sight. At the end of 1914, the Ansaldo group, one of the country's largest manufacturing holding companies, created the Banca Italiana di Sconto which immediately became the third credit bank in the country. This was a very dangerous initiative, as can be seen from its eventual unfortunate outcome, but not an exceptional one. Faced with the difficulty of financing large investments with deferred profitability, Ansaldo did not hesitate in trying to gain control of a bank. The ultimate consequences of the tight links between one large industrial firm and one large bank were seen after the War with the failure of the latter and the call upon the state to support the former.

Economic policy

Crispi's resignations were followed by a period of uncertainty and political instability characterized by essentially reactionary pressure. After 1900, however, there was a turn towards liberal politics more able to cope with the features of a society in which the effects of industrial growth were beginning to make themselves felt: in particular, the widening and modernization of the bourgeoisie and the strengthening of workers' organizations. The greater articulation being acquired by Italian society was reflected in the numerous pressures and counter-pressures which Giolitti tried to balance with 'a system of government bent on carrying out a programme of the Left within the conservative framework provided by the state apparatus, which [acted] as counterweight, as a guarantee that it was kept under strict control.'[40]

Economic policy was part of this picture and this climate. The attitude to the question of tariffs appears rather typical. The 1887

117

Tariff Act was in force throughout the period, almost as if to reassure the agriculturalists, steel and cotton industrialists who had promoted it and to whom it remained as necessary as ever. At the same time, however, there were attempts to satisfy other emerging interests with *ad hoc* legislation as well as with customs treaties: an example of the former being the 1903 measure which allowed duty free importation of steel products used as input for engineering products destined for export. Even though this measure came rather late, the disadvantages of Italian producers in foreign markets were finally eliminated. More complex is the evaluation of the customs treaties. Those signed between 1904–6 with Austria-Hungary, Switzerland and Germany are held to have strengthened the defence of products other than cereals.[41] As regards the steel industry these treaties resulted in a modest lowering of the duty paid on average for every tonne imported.[42]

One important aspect of economic policy in the Age of Giolitti was the impulse given to the creation of social overhead capital, especially in railways. The regime established by the 1885 law produced, as always happens in such cases, a slowing down of investments on the part of the concessionary companies in the light of the expiry date of the concession, after twenty years. This had negative effects on the quality of the service offered, which was not improved by the railway workers' strikes for wage improvements which the companies had no reason to grant, given that their concessions would soon expire. Considerable pressure was put on the government by users and workers alike for the concessions not to be renewed. In July 1905 the state assumed direct control of the railways, with the exception of those run by the Società per le strade ferrate meridionali on a network of about 2,000 kilometres of its own property. Negotiations for the acquisition of this dragged on until the following year when a resolution was passed in parliament for its redemption. Nationalization saw the beginning of a third railway boom which was based mainly on the replacement of obsolete equipment and on technical improvements.[43] Investment in this and other public works sectors appears, *ex post*, as one of the important contributions of economic policy to growth during the Giolitti era.[44]

Monetary and budget policies were closely linked after 1861.[45] The period 1899–1909 was the only one in Italy's history from the Unification to the present day in which the state budget showed[46] a surplus of revenue over actual state expenditure with an absolute increase in both accompanied by a fall in their ratio to national income from 14 to 12 per cent between 1896 and 1907 (or from 19 to 14 per cent if one takes into account local authority and National

Insurance expenditure, net of transfers between them and the state).[47] A balanced budget was one of the policy goals of the governments.[48] It was certainly helped by the increase in revenue deriving from the growth of income, but it is likely that it had, in its turn, created a *mix* of financial and monetary conditions such as to contribute to the support of growth itself.

The reduction of the public debt favoured the allocation of financial resources to private investment expenditure at a moment in which the latter's performance was particularly lively.[49] Moreover, given the prevailing theories on public finance during this period, an 'orthodox' budgetary policy had beneficial effects on the expectations of Italian and foreign businessmen. In one of the first articles of a long series containing ever more favourable comments on the financial situation in Italy, *The Economist* wrote in 1903 'the great need of the present moment in Italy is not only to safeguard her strong financial position, but to reduce and redistribute taxation in such a way as to promote the industry and the social welfare of the people.'[50] A few years later the comment was even more explicit: 'the Italian Budget statement presents . . . a refreshing contrast to the ingenious but hasty expedients by which the French Budget has been made to balance, and still more to the load of a new debt and fresh taxation which the German Empire is piling on an unwilling but impotent people.'[51] This climate of renewed confidence in the financial stability of the country was further increased by the prudence of the banks of issue which, freed from the constant worry of having to provide large loans to the Treasury, did not find it difficult to meet the reserve requirements established by the Bank Act of 1893 and to accumulate gold in excess of them. Between 1900 and 1906 metallic cover of currency rose from 48.5 to 73.6 per cent.

The Bank of Italy in these years had to strike a balance between its private banking enterprise nature and its new role as Central Bank. The first required a large accumulation of profits and the setting aside of liquid reserves against the tied up assets inherited from the liquidation of the Banca Romana. As Central Bank it had to guarantee the stability of prices and exchange rates, as well as provide enough liquidity for a rapidly expanding economy.[52] Compatibility between these objectives did not present particular problems until 1905.

The policy of decreasing interest rates dictated by considerations of a 'business' nature in a situation of high liquidity of the economy and keen banking competition [was] in line with the opportunity to contribute to financing the expansion in the system's productive capacity, and did not risk jeopardising the situation of foreign exchange rates, which was in clear and progressive improvement. Between 1899 and 1905, the average annual exchange rate on Paris fell from 107.32 to 99.94; that in London from 27.07 to 25.14.[53]

The fall in interest rates, which depended partly on the situation of public finance was sanctioned by the conversion of the 5 per cent Italian Consols (Rendita Italiana). This operation, of which there had already been talk in 1902, was included in the Giolitti government's programme in 1903 without the announcement disturbing share prices, thus showing the existence of already consolidated expectations of a reduction in interest rates. In June 1906, Parliament decided to offer Consols holders[54] the option either of reimbursement at par value or of conversion into a new unredeemable bond yielding 3.75 per cent. The operation had considerable success both in Italy and abroad. Of 8,100 million lire, the overall outstanding stock of securities to be converted, only 4.7 million lire were reimbursed and 48.8 million lire were purchased by the *ad hoc* consortia of banks that had been set up in order to avoid undesired falls in prices.

From 1906 onwards the drop in stocks and shares prices and the crisis of the Società Bancaria Italiana posed new problems for the Bank of Italy which, having weathered the 1907 emergency, now found itself in a situation in which the compatibility between monetary objectives imposed difficult choices.[55] The cooling down of domestic demand, especially in investments, and the growing requirements of the Treasury after 1910 and again during the Italo-Turkish war required an accommodating attitude in the supply of liquidity to the system, while the need to defend exchange rates and the banks' gold reserves pushed in the opposite direction, favouring a rise in interest rates. On the whole, the second need prevailed and monetary policy tended in these years to be rather restrictive with a fall in the ratio of currency circulation to national income.[56] This choice probably had some influence on the difficulties of long-term finance complained of by big business, to which Stringher was not insensitive foreseeing the need to ease the legal limits on currency circulation.

Development and regional imbalances

The dualistic nature of Italy's economy has been touched on briefly, but further reference must be made to the regional imbalances of Italy's economic system for two reasons. The first can be traced back to the great vigour which the debate on the 'southern question' assumed from the 1890s onwards. The second regards the presumed widening of interregional income gaps during this relatively long period of agricultural and industrial growth.

The 'southern question' attracted some of the best minds in the country: Nitti, Villani, Colajanni, Fortunato, Salvemini, De Viti-De Marco, and Einaudi. While space does not permit even a brief reference to the tone of the debate and to the numerous historical, political, and economic studies of the time, one must recall the position of the free-traders, fierce opponents of the 1887 Tariff Act who saw in protectionism the principal cause of most of Italy's ills among which was the rise of the great monopolies in the north to the detriment of the promising southern export industries and the strengthening, with the duty on grain, of the conservative interests of the south. This was more or less the position of those who gathered around Salvemini's weekly magazine L'Unità. For Nitti, the south played the role within Italy that the colonies had played elsewhere: that of an exploitation market for raw materials (in this case mainly agricultural) and an outlet for northern manufacturers. In his opinion, the reasons for this were to be found more in the political manner in which the Risorgimento had taken place than in purely economic factors. This position was, in fact, later taken up by Antonio Gramsci. There were others, such as Fortunato, who assumed more eclectic positions and who did not fail to give as one of the causes of the backwardness of the south 'structural' factors such as the scarcity of resources (above all water), the orographic characteristics of the country and the distance from the more highly developed areas of Europe.

This great flourishing of ideas and interpretations has not been supported – either then or later – by an adequate commitment to quantitative analysis. There have been serious studies made in this field: the names of Bachi and Mortara should suffice to recall that the most penetrating economic statisticians of the time devoted much interest to the 'southern question' and it is certain that without their contribution we would know very litle about the actual terms of the problem. However, the quantitative support of the individual explanations of the backwardness of the south remains asystematic and sketchy. The most complete study to date is that by Zamagni who used the rich supply of information contained in the 1911 Industrial Census[57] to try to measure the dimensions of the interregional economic gap just before the First World War.

As can be seen in Table 10.4, per capita income in the southern provinces was almost always less than half that of Liguria, in 1911

Table 10.4 Regional economic indicators in 1914

Region	Per capita income	Industrial value added per worker
Northern		
Piemonte	79	88
Liguria	100	100
Lombardia	73	96
Veneto	63	62
Emilia	47	80
Central		
Toscana	48	71
Marche	38	61
Umbria	33	63
Lazio	53	88
Southern		
Abruzzi	23	49
Campania	43	57
Puglia	35	58
Basilicata	19	49
Calabria	17	43
Sicilia	30	49
Sardegna	39	55
National average	57	70

Source: V. Zamagni, *Industrializzazionee squilibri regionali in Italia*, Bologna: Il Mulino, 1978, pp. 194–5 and 198–9.

the most developed area of the country. The gap in industrial labour productivity was even more marked: Basilicata, Calabria and the Abruzzi barely reached a fifth of the Ligurian figure. Since economic growth means above all growth in productivity there is confirmation here of the fact that the process of industrialization produced an increase in the regional gap in per capita income. It is likely therefore that the south's economic position had been deteriorating during the Giolittian phase of rapid industrialization, despite the undoubted progress made by the south itself in the same period. It is not difficult to assume that an acceleration of economic growth realized in a situation of moderate dualism tends to make the phenomenon more acute. This experience is common to the various processes of modern economic growth[58] and may be explained with the operating of positive externalities affecting factors' productivity in a region that is even *moderately* more advanced than another. Territorial re-equilibrium, in the absence of state intervention, takes place only when the above-mentioned externalities become negative. It is highly probable that these market mechanisms provide a better explanation of the widening of the gap in per capita income between north and south than does either protectionism or the 'colonialist' attitude of the Piedmontese ruling class.

Chapter eleven

The War economy

The economic problems of the First World War

For an economic system war poses allocation and distribution problems of hitherto unknown proportions since it may rely only in a very limited way on obtaining the necessary resources through growth in GDP. This is due in part to the quantity of goods and services necessary for waging war and in part because war itself makes the increase in income through growth in production factors more difficult. With general conscription a large part of the work force has to be removed from production, and those industries hitherto producing capital goods have to devote much of their energy to war production. Thus, as Einaudi noted, 'the economic problem of the conduct of war lay in the changing of the ratio between public goods and private goods in the distribution of the flow of social income.'[1] This process of resource reallocation, contrary to the predictions of politicians, General Staff, and economists, turned out to be of colossal dimensions and had, moreover, to be carried out in a very limited period of time. Actual government expenditure which in Italy, during the twenty years before the First World War, had remained at between 10 and 15 per cent of gross national income, with a falling trend during the first decade of the twentieth century, rose to 59 per cent in 1918.[2]

Given this state of affairs, the methods used in this enormous reallocation process – which permitted the necessary changes in production in order to meet the demand created by the War – were anything but neutral, neither as far as productive efficiency and the personal distribution of income during the War itself were concerned nor as regards the path of development to be followed once hostilities ceased. Until the end of the eighteenth century the main instruments of reallocation of resources to war purposes had been of a coercive nature, such as requisitioning, corvées, forced labour, or looting. The latter was the normal way of supplying the armies operating in enemy territory until the Napoleonic wars, but might also be used by troops operating in friendly areas. During the First World War requisitioning continued, but given the dimensions and duration of the hostilities its importance was minimal. Corvées and forced labour were replaced, on a large scale, with forms of control of the labour markets. However, in the period 1914–18 the reallocation of resources to the state for war purposes took place mainly through taxation, public debt, and money supply. Each belligerent power used a different *mix* of these expedients.[3] Einaudi maintained that if 'the war is conducted with a gradual increase in taxes so that these cover actual total cost . . . the price level will not grow on average, since the quantity of goods demanded does not change given the fact purchasing power has simply been transferred, without growing, from private consumers to the state.'[4] Another advantage of taxation over other methods of financing war expenditure was seen in the possibility of graduating in as fair a way as possible the sacrifices imposed on private citizens by the war itself. On the other hand, a rapid increase in taxes was likely to produce a fall in production efficiency by removing incentives. Some objected also on ethical grounds: since the generation fighting the War made such great sacrifices, it seemed right that future generations bear at least part of the costs involved in the conflict. Public debt was seen a tool for such intertemporal transfer in that it provided those bearing the physical and moral strain of the War with purchasing power over future resources (national income) which would be produced in peace time. In this way incentives to increase productive effort would be maintained. To the objection that the public debt had inflationary effects it was countered that, in theory, this was not a necessary consequence, even if, in effect, the increasing uncertainty connected with the War could only produce a preference for short and very short-term Treasury bonds which, in a crisis of confidence, would make monetization of the debt inevitable. This likely outcome would in itself produce inflationary expectations and, therefore, inflationary effects. No-one explicitly favoured inflation as an instrument of war financing but it was understood that the implicit 'tax' connected with rising prices enjoyed considerable political advantages: it could be collected easily – requiring neither parliamentary approval nor bureaucratic apparatus – and in the short term would probably gain the maximum social consensus. For a government which has to obtain a large quantity of resources in a short period of time inflation has an obvious appeal.

Production

The growth of around 30 per cent in Italy's GDP between 1914 and 1918 was mostly determined by the huge increase in the wages and salaries of state employees whose numbers had swollen as a result of mobilization. The relevant variable is, therefore, the physical output of the agricultural and industrial sectors.

During the War Italian agriculture produced on average more or less the same quantity of goods as in the period 1908–12.[5] Taking into account the fact that the nucleus of the army was formed of peasants – 2.6 million males over the age of 18 were removed from the agricultural labour force[6] – there was a substantial growth in output per worker.

Manufacturing output grew by 30 per cent in 1915, as compared to the previous year, remained constant in 1916, and fell in 1917 and 1918 when, however, it was still more than 8 per cent above the average for the period 1908–13.

If taken as a whole the quantitative performance of the Italian manufacturing industry during the War appears anything but insignificant, much more important are the transformation of the production *mix* and of the rate of technical progress. One of the main criticisms of pre-War industrial policy focused on the scant attention paid to the engineering and chemical sectors, industries in which Italy had a potential comparative advantage. The fact that the conflict immediately appeared as a 'war . . . of raw materials and industry'[7] obliged the government to devote great attention to promoting the development of these two key industries. Reliable estimates of value added by the various manufacturing sectors during the War are not available, but the indications that can be drawn from existing information on individual sectors and businesses leave no doubts as to the magnitude of their growth. 'The initially low level of artillery equipment rose, by the end of the war, to 7,709 cannons (as against the 6,690 of England and the 11,608 of France) and that of machine-guns from 613 to 19,904.'[8] 'In the period from 1913–14 to 1918–19 the Navy ordered the building of 572 ships'[9] and the effort was much greater for the production of merchant ships of which 180,000 tonnes were launched. 'The production of automobiles rose from 9,200 units in 1914 to 20,000 in 1918, while large scale construction of trucks and tractors for military use was begun and an active export system was nourished.'[10] By the end of the War the aeronautical industry, virtually non-existent in 1913, employed 100,000 workers.[11] 'The chemical industry, freed from the competition of superior German technology, reduced its production for civil consumption, especially fertilizers, but increased more than proportionally that of raw materials for explosives[12] even though substantial imports were still required. The engineering and chemical industries were destined to play an important role in the country's development during the following half century.

The long run results of war-time investments were of two types. Where the new investments could be converted at low costs to the production of non-military goods the result was an overall increase in the country's productive capacity: this was particularly true in the case of the aeronautical, automobile, and rubber industries. Where, on the other hand, conversion costs were high, as in the case of armaments, or where an excess capacity had been created, as in the case of the shipbuilding industry once submarine warfare had come to an end and once the average life of the fleet had been lengthened, war investments constituted essentially a net loss of wealth.

The demand for war products and the way in which its production was financed gave rise to, or consolidated, a number of large enterprises which would play a crucial role in Italy's industrial history for many decades to come. One need only mention FIAT, which had just emerged from a crisis, that had threatened its survival, ILVA, Breda, Montecatini, and Pirelli. The most unusual case was that of Ansaldo, the old Genoese firm which had been among the first in Italy to build locomotives and control of which was now assumed by the Perrone brothers. In 1914, the total value of its output was estimated at 215 million lire, with 56,000 employees. By 1919 it had reached 2,000 million lire with a total of 111,000 employees.[13] The growth of the Ansaldo group, aided by the creation in 1914 of the Banca Italiana di Sconto, with which it had close links, depended chiefly on the war orders placed with its many subsidiary companies operating in the steel, engineering, electromechanical, naval, aeronautical, and maritime transport sectors. Peace brought about a major crisis in the entire concern which was able to survive only by becoming the first large state-owned manufacturing company in Italy, more than a decade before the creation of IRI.

The organization of production

In theory, the rapid reallocation process required by the War could be left entirely to the market, once suitable financial means (taxes, debt, currency circulation) had been found to give the state adequate power of command over real resources. In practice, without direct allocative action by the state it was likely that bottlenecks would arise creating delays in supply while there was general agreement that 'the time factor must have precedence over any other considerations.'[14]

Therefore, one month after Italy had entered the War (24 May 1915), the Institute of Mobilization was created in order to allow the government

> to oblige entrepreneurs to undertake those investments that would increase the productive capacity of private factories . . . to requisition for serious and urgent necessities part of the electrical energy destined for public services and private use . . . to force the construction and supply of material necessary for war use, at prices established by the industrialists themselves and, in case of excessive requests, by the military administration itself with the possibility of appeal to an arbitration board. . . . Later, it was also established that . . . the Ministry responsible would be able to take decisions independently of the owners and assume direct management control (of the firms).[15]

To make these orders operative a Supreme Committee of Ministers was formed as well as an Under-Secretariate for Arms and Munitions[16] which, in June 1917, became a Ministry. For almost the entire duration of the conflict General Alfredo Dallolio was head of this administration and he succeeded in becoming that 'dictator of the economic conduct of the war that had been asked for in various quarters'.[17] A new bureaucracy was thus created, organized in regional committees, to give hundreds of private firms orders for war materials, clothing, and foodstuffs destined for the army. The firms deemed suitable were declared 'auxiliaries' and were subject to military supervision. Einaudi notes that

> the advantages for the industrialists of being enrolled on the auxiliary list were great: exemptions from conscription meant they were able to get all the men they needed for war production; the workers thus obtained could be subjected to a rigorous discipline along military lines; strikes and workers' unrest were suppressed; wage and working conditions could be fixed by the arbitration board of the regional mobilization committees.[18]

There were 215 auxiliary factories at the end of 1915, 932 a year later and 1,976 by the end of the War; 60 per cent were concentrated in 'the industrial triangle and only 16 per cent in southern Italy and the islands.'[19]

In order to make the carrying out of orders and contracts easier they were no longer subject to scrutiny on the part of the State Auditors' Department; the industrialists were given large cash advances and rapid payments for their products; the supply of raw materials was eased as much as possible. Inevitably this bureaucratized and centralized organization, which was at the same time freed from the procedures and controls typical of the meticulous peacetime bureaucracy, lent itself to the many abuses reported by newspapers and the records of the Parliamentary Inquiry Commission on War Expenditure.[20] The system undoubtedly allowed some firms to make exceptional profits, favouring the larger ones whose contractual capacity was stronger, given that they were relied on as indispensable for steady supplies. Such firms also succeeded in obtaining priority for supplies of raw materials, an element which would become more important with the prolongation of hostilities.[21] These circumstances produced strong incentives for mergers and vertical integration of firms, the most resounding example of this being the Ansaldo group.

The state also intervened in the supplies of raw materials which were mostly imported. Common foodstuffs were rationed both in order to avoid an apparent inequality in basic consumption likely to lead to social discontent and, possibly to a drop in the War effort and to guarantee priority in supplying the combat troops with large amounts of food. Cereals and livestocks destined for the slaughterhouse were requisitioned and a system of grain stockpiling was created and financed by the state, and run in such a way as to fix a ceiling for prices and guarantee as fair a distribution as possible. Price control was extended to other goods and gradually a rationing system was organized. The continuation of the submarine war made the problems of supplies, in 1917, even more acute and therefore it was decided at first to advise and then, in October, to impose the adoption of ration cards. They were abolished at the armistice, reintroduced shortly afterwards and only definitively suppressed in June 1921. In Einaudi's opinion, the system turned out to be rather efficient and it met with considerable popular favour which would have been greater had there not been suspicions of favouritism and if, indeed, it had not turned out to be impossible to force rationing on the peasants.

The financing of the War

Actual state expenditure, equal to 2.8 billion lire in 1913, rose to 30.8 billion in the tax year ending on 30 June 1919. Allowing for inflation, government expenditure rose by 350 per cent in real terms.

About a quarter of overall state expenditure between 1915 and 1919 was financed by taxation.[22] The remainder was covered by loans and by currency issue. Between 1915 and 1918 five large national War Loans were issued. The first three consisted of long-term bonds (with maturities of not fewer than ten and no more than twenty-five years); their yields increased slightly with each issue. The last two issues (January 1917 and January 1918) were, in practice, consolidated loans. In the period 1915–1919 these issues yielded 13.7 billion lire, net of conversions of single bonds into later issues. The uncertainties about war operations and inflation led dealers to prefer shorter-term bonds: pluriennial and annual Treasury bills. The large issue of such bills, used before the War only in order to cover temporary cash imbalances of the Treasury, were a sort of 'financial innovation' introduced by the War. In the period 1915–19 Treasury bills for 14.7 billion lire were issued. At the end of the War, almost 60 per cent of the outstanding debt was made up of short- and medium-term bonds. Since term structure of public debt was undesirable because of its likely inflationary impact, a large 'consolidated loan' was launched in January 1920 at conditions attractive to the holders of Treasury Bills of which about 40 per cent were converted into Consols.

From July 1915 to June 1919 two-thirds of all public expenditure was financed by means of taxes or debt. What remained was covered by direct loans on current account from the banks of issue to the state: in practice by an increase in currency circulation. After the suspension of gold payments in August 1914 various parliamentary bills raised the limits on the amounts that the banks of issue were obliged to lend the state.

The role of the three banks of issue in war-finance was not limited to loans to the Treasury. Sraffa has noted that 'for the duration of the war, in Italy and abroad, governments pushed for increases in bank credit in order to favour their own war loans.'[23] With this aim in mind, the banks of issue granted advances on Treasury bonds to credit institutions and firms on particularly favourable terms. Moreover, the banks of issue financed the so-called 'Grain consortia' and provided savings banks and other minor banks with whatever liquidity was needed in order to avoid their selling the state bonds held in their portfolios on the market whenever a confidence crisis arose. In the context of war financing, the Consorzio Sovvenzioni su Valori Industriali (CVSI) should be mentioned, mostly for the importance it acquired during the 1920s. The Consortium, made up of the three banks of issue, savings banks, and a few other credit firms, came into being on 20 December 1914. Its aim was to allow the discount of commercial papers with one signature[24] against the security of industrial shares and bonds, of imported raw materials and later manufactures, as well as the discount of promisory notes issued by official warehouses, and of industrial bills of exchange with two or more signatures.[25] The Consortium, in turn, financed its operations by rediscounting those bills[26] with the banks of issue. During the War these operations were very contained (47 million lire in 1918),[27] but the Consortium's importance was increased considerably in the post-war years.

Prices, exchange rates, and the balance of payments

It is likely that the strong expansion in money supply was the main cause of Italy's high inflation rate. The index of wholesale prices in Italy grew faster than that of all the countries included in Table 11.1, especially from 1916–17 onwards when the War effort was greater and later still with the defeat at Caporetto. Administrative controls and the introduction of ration cards did not succeed in checking the inflation rate which was 49 per cent – much higher than Germany's 21 per cent rate.

Table 11.1   Wholesale price indices 1914–19

Year	Italy	France	U.K.	Germany	Spain	Holland	Sweden
1914	100	100	100	100	100	100	100
1915	130	135	122	124	120	135	144
1916	190	182	158	147	142	206	183
1917	285	252	205	169	168	232	242
1918	425	329	227	205	207	262	336
1919	465	341	251	393	207	265	328

Source: B.R. Mitchell, *European Historical Statistics 1750–1950*, London: Macmillan, 1975, pp. 390–1.

Given such a tendency in domestic prices relative to those in the other leading belligerent and neutral countries and the growing deficit on foreign current accounts, the success obtained in limiting the devaluation of the external value of the lira, due above all to the financial solidarity established among the allies of the *Entente*, appears even greater.

During the Giolitti years, the disequilibrium in the balance of trade was covered by 'invisible' items, mainly emigrants' remittances and tourism. These items virtually dried up during the War while the disequilibrium in the balance of trade grew enormously.

Exports covered 75 per cent of imports in 1914, 55 per cent in 1915 and only 20 per cent in the last year of the War.

From 1914 on measures were introduced for a regulation of the foreign exchange markets. In December 1917 the National Institute for foreign exchange was created and was given the monopoly in dealing in foreign currencies. It began operations the following March. The Institute was organized by a consortium of the three banks of issue, as well as the Banca Commerciale, Credito Italiano, the Banca Italiana di Sconto, and the Banco di Roma. Its chairman was Stringher, General Manager of the Bank of Italy. Throughout the War the authorities' intervention on the foreign exchange markets aimed at keeping the lira slightly over-valued relative to its purchasing power parity. Its devaluation against the pound was slowly steered from the pre-War rate of 25 lire to 31–32 lire around which it oscillated in 1915–16. In 1917 there was a further slide to 34 and 35 lire and a leap to 41 at the time of the defeat at Caporetto. After August 1918, when victory was close at hand, the lira revalued rapidly, going from 43 to 30.4 (average for November). Apart from fluctuations due to uncertainty regarding War operations, after an initial devaluation the lira remained relatively stable on the London market for the duration of the War. This was made possible by the large amounts of official credit obtained by Italy, first from the British government and, later, from Washington for the purchase of goods on those markets and, within certain limits, also on those of neutral countries. At the end of the War, the final amount of Italian foreign debt was 20.6 billion gold lire,[28] equal to more than seven-times the value of Italian exports in 1918.[29]

Chapter twelve

The economic development of Liberal Italy: some interpretations

Some, among the many, 'facts in search of a theory'

The choice of the facts described so far has privileged those which seem to the author to be most important for an understanding of the Italian industrialization process in the social and political context of Liberal Italy between the Peace of Villafranca and the Treaty of Versailles. This process has been taken to be synonymous with Kuznets' modern economic growth. The 'when and how' has been discussed (mainly, but not only, in the chapters devoted to quantitative analysis) in an essentially factual way. Frequent reference has been made to important problems of interpretation, but they have not been dealt with in a complete or systematic fashion. The time has now come to see how some important facts may move in search of an explanatory theory.

The central issue is that of the 'peculiarity' of Italy's development. Given that each single 'case' has its own peculiarities, scholars have tended to see them in the light of 'historical models' or of theoretical frames. One typical question is the following: are the most significant analogies to be found in the process of English industrialization (and in part with that of France), in the growth of 'latecomers' such as Germany, Russia, and Japan, or in a 'Mediterranean case' which has yet to be perfectly identified? Other specific questions which have fascinated historians deal with the causes of the economic stagnation in the thirty years after the Unification; the typical features of the rapid development during the Giolotti years; the origins and deepening of the dualism between the south and the rest of the country; the effects of economic policies and, in particular, of customs tariffs. These are broad historical problems to which economics may provide only limited answers: for instance, the fact of being able to define a 'Liberal Italy' chronologically, which was followed by Fascist dictatorship, has posed in an overall and dramatic way the basic question of the social and

133

political failure of the regime created as a result of the Risorgimento. Any question regarding the origins of Fascism must take into consideration the characteristics of accumulation and growth during the so-called Liberal period, thus shedding new light on the 'peculiarity' of Italian economic growth during those years.

What follows will be a necessarily brief account of the search for explanations of those facts which have aroused greatest interest. Although the discussion will deal mainly with economic issues, reference will inevitably have to be made to a general and far more complex picture on which historians' opinion is still very much divided.

Backwardness, growth, and accumulation: Gramsci and Romeo

One of the first important facts requiring explanation in the Italian case of modern economic growth regards the chronology of this growth as a starting point for an analysis of its causes.

First of all, one has to understand both the stagnation in per capita income during the first three decades following the Unification and its subsequent rapid rise in the following twenty years. The Marxian idea, appropriated by much Tory historiography in England, that an agricultural revolution – seen as a necessary condition for capital accumulation – must necessarily precede an industrial revolution has been applied to the analysis of the Italian case by historians of both Marxist and Liberal inspiration. Among the former, the most important reference is to Gramsci. This is not an easy task because he wrote while imprisoned in a Fascist jail and his work was of necessity asystematic, thus presenting not a few difficulties of interpretation. It seems, however, safe to say that according to Gramsci the unsatisfactory realization of the economic promises of the Risorgimento had its origin in the lack of an agricultural revolution. This was the result of the inability of the moderate Right, which had led the political movement towards Unification, to promote a complete democratic–bourgeois revolution and conquer, through an alliance with the peasant masses, a complete social hegemony after having eliminated the remains of feudalism still existing in most rural areas, particularly in the south.[1]

Gramsci, in an authentically Marxian way, does not disguise his nostalgia for a hegemonic bourgeoisie and a strong capitalist development – the premiss for social changes which would ultimately lead to socialism – of which he saw too feeble a trace in post-Risorgimento Italy. The model of reference (seen in England's first industrial revolution by Marx) was, for Gramsci, revolutionary

France where the alliance between bourgeoisie and peasants would have been cemented by a distribution of land to the latter. This is, therefore, an essentially political interpretation of the term 'agricultural revolution' although Gramsci maintains that in France this did not fail to achieve the classic objectives of an increase in production and productivity which lead to original accumulation. The breaking up of the great landed estates (Gramsci was particularly interested in the political outcome on the balance of power between hegemonic classes) implied an increase in productivity as much of land as of labour since he seems to maintain that the creation of small peasant-owned farms does not fail to have considerable effects on the whole system of incentives. The greatest interpreter of the Gramscian tradition, Emilio Sereni, has added a very important element:[2] that relating to the slow formation of a unified national market which, in the absence of a true agricultural revolution, remained too limited. There were therefore, difficulties in the development of manufacturing industry which had to defend its oligopolistic positions and rely more than elsewhere on state support, granted in various forms.

This way of interpreting the unsatisfactory behaviour of the Italian economy after the Unification – more intuited than quantified since neither Gramsci nor Sereni had national accounting statistics at their disposal – has been widely criticized. It has been said that the national and international conditions necessary for the radical realization of a democracy founded on the alliance of the bourgeoisie and the peasants did not exist in Italy during the 1850s and 1860s. However, this would not invalidate the economic content of Gramsci's thesis; it would only shift its causes from a presumed timidness of the Italian bourgeoisie to the political, social and diplomatic context in which the Risorgimento took place. From a strictly economic point of view, it is more important to ask whether an agricultural revolution based on the creation of owner–occupier small-holdings would have been able to accelerate the growth in national income after the country's Unification. Agricultural economists see in the insufficient size of farms one of the main obstacles to the growth of productivity,[3] nor does it seem easy to assume that a large co-operative movement could have been easily created with appropriate incentives in the Italian south. Moreover, it is difficult to assume that a more egalitarian distribution of property and income would have encouraged the accumulation of capital for industrial development and the complementary movement of labour from the countryside to the cities. On the same socio-political plane, the reactionary ideology prevailing in Italian rural areas, and the French experience, lead one to doubt that an

Italian *paysannerie* would have had a progressive role. Another obstacle to the acceptance of the Gramscian theory lies in the fact that while it explains the economic stagnation of the first thirty years after the Unification it does not shed light on the rapid development of the following twenty, in which there was certainly not an agricultural revolution of the type postulated by Gramsci.

It should be said, however, that Gramsci and those following his views, Sereni first of all, had analytic ambitions far more complex than those attributed to them in the debate between Romeo and Gerschenkron which took place in the second half of the 1950s. They wanted to deal with the main structural problem of the entire post-Unification history: the weakness of the bourgeoisie; and they saw the main cause in the fact that 'Italy's political revolution was not based on an agricultural revolution.'[4] However, on closer examination, a more important economic issue would seem to be that of studying the effects of this weakness rather than explaining its causes.

> The incompleteness of the bourgeois revolution in Italy would not only have important political consequences, leaving the way open to recurrent attacks on the part of the old dominating classes, and maintaining their influence in the political life of the country and in the state machinery itself; but was to be at the root of all the difficulties and all the internal contradictions of Italian capitalism, until very recently, intensifying and aggravating them. The remains of feudalism . . . would make Italy a typical economic latecomer. . . . For many years to come one would be able to say of Italy what Marx said about the Germany of his time: that 'it suffered both from capitalism and from an insufficient development of the same.'[5]

This is an overall interpretation of the economic and social history of the country which presents many plausible elements on a factual ground and goes much beyond the discussion of the possible productivity and accumulation gains deriving from an agricultural revolution of the kind which according to Gramsci had taken place in revolutionary France.

In antithesis to Gramsci, Romeo starts from an optimistic view of the results obtained by the Liberal revolution. His interpretation of the chronology of Italian growth is based on a mix of the classical view of an agricultural revolution as prerequisite for an industrial revolution and of the theories of economic development accepted in the 1950s. According to Romeo, 'the challenge facing the participants in the Risorgimento, which they met in the most consistent way, given the constraints inherent in the Italian situation, was to proceed to a forced strengthening of the urban capitalist economy of the north and to the unification of the market, as indispensable premises for the transformation of southern rural areas.'[6] According to Romeo, the 1860s and 1870s witnessed a substantial accumulation in agriculture. The resources thus created, however, were first – and quite rightly – used for the creation of social overhead capital, first of all railways, as a necessary prerequisite for profitability of private investment. Once the first phase of creating a basic railway network was over, in the 1880s, the surplus generated by agriculture found its way to industry. Romeo accepts in part the Gramscian arguments on the weakness of the Italian bourgeoisie: 'certainly the whole process took place for a long time on a basis of compromise with the semi-feudal elements of the old agrarian world, especially in the South',[7] but, on the whole, economic growth got under way. This implied 'development of the city at the expense of the countryside, growth in the North at the expense of the South',[8] but these are both temporary and necessary conditions for every process of industrialization.

Romeo found support for his thesis, which is consistent with the behaviour of the index of industrial production, in the national accounting statistics then just issued by ISTAT,[9] from which he gained the impression that agricultural production rose considerably between 1861 and 1880, finding in this confirmation of the existence of an agricultural revolution able to generate a sort of original accumulation. Unfortunately, Romeo's interpretation of those data was incorrect and subsequent revisions point to the opposite direction: what is known about Italian agriculture leads one to believe that it made little progress between 1861 and 1880. At the same time Fenoaltea's recent research shows that investments in public works and railways grew substantially from the 1880s onwards.

On a theoretical level too, there are difficulties in accepting Romeo's explanation of the time path of Italy's development. The very idea of the necessity of an agricultural revolution appears obsolete. On the other hand, the explanation of the time lag between the creation of social overhead capital and industrialization is not convincing. If one holds that industrial growth was constrained only by lack of capital supply, it is not easy to understand why the widening of the market through the creation of railways is considered to be so important. If, on the other hand, one emphasizes the size of aggregate demand – for example, because economies of scale are held to be crucial – there is no real reason

137

why industry should not grow side by side with the fall in transport costs produced by the railways. This said, it should be added that Romeo must be credited with having proposed an interpretative scheme based on an explanatory theory which aimed to be empirically verifiable. Even now his work constitutes an important methodological reference point. Romeo is one of the most articulate interpreteters of the Liberal historical tradition and his exemplary biography of Cavour has often been referred to in this volume. His interpretation of Italian economic growth, besides the analytic and factual questions it raises, contains a view of the period which, together with that of Gramsci and Sereni, with whom he ends up having more points of contact than the author would like to admit − has been a point of reference for an entire generation of historians.

Gerschenkron's relative backwardness hypothesis

Italy is an important case study used by Gerschenkron to illustrate his well-known general proposition that 'in a number of important historical instances the industrialization process, when launched at length in a backward country, showed considerable differences, as compared with more advanced countries, not only with regard to the speed of the development (the rate of industrial growth) but also with regard to the productive and organizational structures of industry which emerged from those processes.'[10]

According to Gerschenkron, only rather advanced countries, as England certainly was in the eighteenth century, followed the 'classical' model of development based on the accumulation of capital in agriculture and on a process of transfer of resources to industry taking place by virtue of market forces alone. In this case, industrial development is rather slow, does not present important discontinuities and depends mostly on growth in the demand for consumer goods.

More backward countries on the Continent, with the possible exception of France, tended to diverge from the 'classical' model of industrialization. Backwardness creates 'a tension between the actual state of the economic activities in the country and the existing obstacles to industrial development on the one hand, and the great promise inherent in such a development on the other.'[11] Backward European economies were characterized by low productivity in agriculture, low savings ratios, shortage of skilled labour and entrepreneurial talents, hostility to social changes that are both a requirement for and a consequence of modern economic growth, and by the inability and unwillingness of the majority of political leaders to favour such changes. When the 'promise' of industrial development is sufficiently large, a backward country resorts to substitutes for the classical 'prerequisites' of industrialization (such as original accumulation in agriculture). The necessary reallocation of resources to industrial ventures takes place by virtue of 'agents of industrialization' able to sustain and strengthen otherwise weak market forces. Such a role was played by the 'mixed' or 'universal' banks in the case of moderately backward countries (such as Germany and Italy) and by the state in the case of very backward countries (the Balkans and Russia). In order to compete with already developed economies, the backward country adopts modern labour-saving technologies in some key sectors such as metal-making, and advanced engineering and chemical productions. The role of the above-mentioned 'agents' is precisely that of favouring resource allocation in the technologically advanced sectors. Hence a rapid 'spurt' of industrialization concentrated in the production of investment goods and characterized by a widespread dualism between modern and traditional sectors.

According to Gerschenkron, Italy had its own 'agents of industrialization' in the German banks, Banca Commerciale, and Credito Italiano, established on the eve of the Giolittian 'big spurt' which – on the basis of his own index of industrial production – he dates from 1896 to 1908. The index also confirmed Gerschenkron's own expectations that, in a latecomer, a 'spurt' of considerable intensity would favour the 'output of producers' goods as against that of consumers' goods.'[12]

At the same time, he ascribes the weaknesses of Italian industrialization to inept government policies (particularly tariff policies); to a time inconsistency between railway building and the 'spurt'; to political and social restlessness; and to an ideological climate not particularly favourable to industry.

Gerschenkron's explanation of the chronology and characteristics of the process of Italian industrialization has the elegance of simplicity and the considerable interest of fitting into a more general vision of the economic history of nineteenth-century Europe. His contribution to the understanding of Italian development was seminal, providing in the 1950s a breath of fresh air in the rather provincial atmosphere of the historiography of this field. Thirty years later, however, the weaknesses of his interpretation should come as no surprise.

Gerschenkron disregards the considerable industrial growth that took place in the 1880s and which is visible in his own index, although to a lesser extent than in Fenoaltea's. Even more striking is his disregard for the problems of financial instability somehow built-in into a system of financial intermediation based on industrial–universal banking, and for the costs either of major financial crises (1888–93) or of lending-of-last-resort operations (1907 and 1911). Moreover, Confalonieri's monumental work[13] (published many years after Gerschenkron's) shows on the one hand that the 'French' banks (Credito Mobiliare and Banca Generale) were not timid promotors of large manufacturing enterprises and, on the other, that the industrial equity held in the portfolios of the two 'German' banks, until 1919, was much less important than Gerschenkron believed (with the probable exception of the electrical sector).

Growth, cycles, and public policy according to Fenoaltea

Fenoaltea's contribution to the debate on the process of Italian industrialization between 1861 and 1913 is one of the most fruitful. His index of industrial production[14] and his recent sectorial studies of monumental precision have already been referred to. Fenoaltea's work is still in progress: the final aim being the construction of a new and much more reliable index to be used as a basis for an overall reconsideration of Italian industrialization during the second half of the last century.

In Fenoaltea's view there were no 'big spurts':[15] Italy's industrial production was normally characterized by cyclical swings 'reflecting the performance of engineering production which in turn moved parallel to the cycle of private demand for durable goods.'[16] The latter was particularly sensitive to profit expectations which Fenoaltea, in his early works,[17] sees as generated by changes in the political climate in favour or against industrial interests producing changes in the perception of investment risks and thus inducing variations in the desired capital/output ratio, reflected in the demand for durable goods produced by the engineering industry.[18]

According to Fenoaltea the agrarian view of the Right made industrialists feel politically powerless and neglected by trade policy,[19] hence the low growth rate of investments and of industrial production until the end of the 1870s. After the 'parliamentary revolution' and the tariff law of 1878,

> the good-will shown by the Depretis administration towards industrial interests seemed to have strengthened business confidence; the gradual improvement in expectations of industrial profit (net of risk) seems to have been the cause of the wave of investment in machinery and equipment which, in turn, was the direct cause of the acceleration of industrial output.[20]

This was clearly visible from 1879 on in Fenoaltea's index. Crispi's first cabinet (1887) 'marked the beginning of a period of politics for politics sake':[21] industry found that Rome was less attentive to its needs. The decline in production, however, was only partially produced by the deterioration in expectations due to the deterioration in the political climate: the rapid growth of the 1880s did not generate large 'multiplier/accelerator effects which would have been able to support it', a reduction in investments was therefore inevitable; however, 'the exogenously induced loss of business confidence doubtless made the depression longer and deeper than it would otherwise have been'.[22] In a similar way, Fenoaltea attributes only part of the Giolittian boom to the effect on entrepreneurial expectations of the third important political change since the Unification; a large part of the cyclical upswing was due to a lagged effect of the preceding political change, transmitted once again by the longevity of investment goods.[23] This is the kernel of Fenoaltea's analysis: a normal cyclical tendency in industrial production, understandable with a simple Harrod–Domar model, had been widened both in the expansion and recession phases by political changes sufficiently radical to induce changes in profit expectations.

> If Depretis' taking over from the Right had not pushed investment demand above the potential output level, the subsequent fall would have been more moderate; if the replacement of Depretis by Crispi had not discouraged investment to an exceptional extent, it would not have been able to bounce back even higher; and if Giolitti had not re-established calm and business confidence the new reflation would not have transformed itself into such rapid development.[24]

This close link between trade cycle and political cycle is not entirely consistent with Fenoaltea's highly critical view of the efficacy of the economic policy of the time. Since each cycle covered a time interval of at least a decade, it is not easy to understand why entrepreneurs did not adapt their own expectations to the disappointing results of government policies. Fenoaltea's average entrepreneur seems to be suffering from 'policy illusion' to an unusual extent, reacting more to parliamentary speeches and to ideological proclamations than to the results of the economic policies actually implemented: his expectations seem neither adaptive nor rational; despite past experience he continues to act – irrationally, given the hypotheses of inefficiency and ineffectiveness of public intervention – on the basis of the prevailing 'ideologico–political climate'

141

of the time. Needless to say, it is not easy to produce a convincing empirical test of this hypothesis. It should be added that Fenoaltea himself believes it to be obsolete and he has recently proposed a different explanation of the Italian industrial cycle.[25] Fenoaltea's new series of investment in construction and public works[26] display a cyclical movement – similar to that of his own previous index of industrial production – which 'seem not population-sensitive but finance-sensitive.'[27] He sees the specific cause of the swings in the supply of *foreign* capital which, in turn, seems related to the long swings in British capital exports.

This interpretation is of particular interest because it aims at suggesting a new unified interpretation of the Atlantic economy 'in which capital flows caused construction, and construction – that employer of labour par excellence – caused migration. In this alternative view the critical distinction is no longer between old lands and new, but that between capital exporters (Britain) and importers (Italy and the New World).'[28]

This new view of the construction cycle will possibly play an important role in Fenoaltea's interpretation of the industrial development of Liberal Italy. However, an overall and fully consistent appraisal of the matter will be made by Fenoaltea only when his new series of industrial output are completed.

The interpretations of Cafagna and Bonelli

Essentially monocausal explanations such as those mentioned so far are attractive by virtue of their simplicity and in that they can be either accepted or rejected on the basis of empirical analysis, but they are more appealing to economists than to historians who mistrust the over-simplification of reality that inevitably results.[29] A more articulate vision of the process of Italian industrialization is that of Cafagna and Bonelli. The former's analysis distinguishes two patterns of growth: that of the so-called traditional sector (textile, in particular silk) and that of a 'modern' or 'new' sector which incorporates the techniques developed in the latter part of the nineteenth century.[30] The traditional sector was characterized by uniform trend acceleration beginning long before the Unification and based on such 'advantages of backwardness' as the agricultural–industrial integration characteristic of silk spinning and the existence of foreign demand coming from already developed countries. As far as the modern sector is concerned, Cafagna agrees in part with Romeo's thesis regarding the role of the state and the importance of market size, but pays little attention to the role of original accumulation.

Neither does Bonelli accept the existence of a discontinuity in 1861,[31] holding it indispensable to go back a few decades to detect the effects produced on Italy's foreign trade by the development of other countries for which Italy was the leading raw material supplier. The resulting growth in income started a slow transformation of the productive structure of the country, which rules out a 'take-off' in the Rostowian sense, and which came to an end only in the second half of the twentieth century. Given the low levels of per capita income and consumption, private demand could not play the role that many claim it played in the so-called 'first industrial revolution' in England. Public demand therefore assumed a more important role than in other countries. Until the beginning of the 1880s the surplus of the balance of payments on current account allowed the payment abroad of interest on the National Debt providing the state with resources for its own organization and for the creation of social overhead capital. There is an analogy here with Romeo's thesis because the trade surplus was due mainly to exports of primary products. With the 'great depression', caused by the competition of American cereals on the European markets, this 'growth model' had, of necessity, to change: the 1887 tariff allowed import substitution to replace exports in sustaining aggregate demand. In the case of the cotton industry, tariff protection was sufficient to generate a fairly steady growth rate. For many of the more 'modern' sectors (in particular steel-making and shipbuilding) state support – provided mainly in the form of government orders and, when necessary, of direct or indirect lending of last resort – was indispensable for sustained growth. Bonelli's analysis is particularly interesting because of the competent way in which it describes the links of implicit collaboration which started around 1900 between the state and the large banks through the mediation of the Bank of Italy. The most solid part of Bonelli's view is, probably that relating to the functioning of the financial market after the banking crisis of the early 1890s. All the rest is plausible, but supported by little empirical analysis: what we know of Italian foreign trade appears absolutely insufficient to prove the important role assigned to it by Bonelli. The same can be said of the trends in the 'traditional' and 'modern' sectors: the research currently being carried out by Fenoaltea will shed entirely new light on this subject.

The role of the government

Much of the debate on Italian economic growth revolves around the role played by the state. Cavour and his followers of the Right, supporters as they were of *laissez-faire*, saw for the government the indispensable role of promoting the creation of social overhead capital, especially where monopolies existed. They saw there a strong case for state ownership of railways, seen as the single most important innovation given the conditions of backwardness and market segmentation existing in 1860. Other than that, the question was whether the best role that the state could play in the historical conditions of Italy in the second half of the nineteenth century was that of 'freeing market forces', that is, guaranteeing producers and consumers an environment free of constraints in which each could maximize profits and utility as the best way to maximize national income, or whether the situation was characterized by 'market failures' which postulated state intervention for a more efficient resource allocation in order to maximize long-term growth.

While travelling in Italy, Cobden, the champion of English free-tradism, 'courteously told D'Azeglio that "Italy's steam is her sun" ';[32] by that he meant that Italy did not have a 'comparative advantage' in manufacturing other than that, such as silk, connected with agriculture. A hundred years later, the same concept was put before the Commissione Economica della Costituente (Parliamentary Economic Commission in charge of drafting the Constitution of the Italian Republic) by textile industrialists. Throughout the century that was to see Italy's transformation from an agricultural country to a modern industrial power, a militant minority of free traders continued to protest against the damage produced by tariffs and by state intervention in general, agreeing that the market is always the best resource allocator and that Italy's comparative advantages were climate and, more importantly, abundance of labour. Left to themselves market forces would produce an economy specialized in products of Mediterranean agriculture and in the labour-intensive manufacturing industries (silk above all, but also wool, cotton, food processing, light engineering, chemical industries, and the like). Exports would buy cheap foreign intermediate and investment goods. On these grounds, the tariff of 1887[33] became the target of harsh attacks.

While not accepting free-tradist dogmatism, Gerschenkron arrives at similar conclusions.

It need not be gainsaid that, at least in principle, Italy's industrialization could have been aided by a rationally conceived and executed tariff. Such policies would have had to start from the basic fact that in a historical period in which coal exercised the main locational pull, a country deprived of the mineral, forced to obtain it (on average) at a price twice as high as that in the coal-mining countries, and thus laboring under the disadvantage of high cost in industry and transportation, should have concentrated on those branches of industrial endeavor in which the expenditure for coal was small in relation to other cost items. Furthermore, a backward country, so disabled, should have felt particularly keenly the need to promote output of new products and new industries. The vast and variegated area of engineering offered the greatest promise in this respect.[34]

What actually happened was exactly the opposite. On the one hand 'the tender plant of (Italy's) industrial growth [was subject] to the rigors of a protectionist climate in agriculture',[35] and on the other, steel-making, the major consumer of coal, was privileged at the expense of engineering. The argument is taken up by Fenoaltea who underlines not so much the insufficient 'effective protection' which prevented the engineering industry from carrying out a meaningful process of import substitution as the disadvantage of Italian engineering exports relative to their competitors. 'Given the high elasticity of supply in the engineering industry and the well-known elasticity in international demand' redressing the disadvantages deriving from the high cost of inputs 'would have opened the way to steady exports and thus to output growth [. . .] and the Crispian depression, attributable to the impossibility of finding remunerative outlets in foreign markets to replace domestic demand which was in rapid contraction, could certainly have been avoided.'[36]

As for Gerschenkron's thesis, it should be said that the effective protection of the engineering industry was never negative, and that the replacement of duty with a subsidy to steel production (so as to avoid the loss of value added in that sector) at best would have raised by 7 per cent, the overall level of industrial production reached in 1908.[37] It is therefore difficult to argue that Italian industrial history would have been significantly different in the presence of a more rational tariff policy. Moreover, doubts remain about the high supply and demand elasticities taken for granted by Fenoaltea. During the boom of the Giolitti years the impression is that of an engineering industry technically unable to adjust its supply to the rapid growth of domestic demand for investment goods. As to the missed opportunity of engineering exports during the slump of the late 1880s, those were times of strong protectionist policies throughout Europe: an attempt to push Italian engineering exports would in all likelihood have met with retaliatory duties.

The most consistent advocates of tariffs and, in general, of state promotion of heavy industry, were to be found among the nationalists, as can be seen from the writings of Filippo Carli.[38] The 'infant industry' argument is certainly advocated, but the basic justification for the protectionist choice are found in each country's need to depend as little as possible on others if it wants to play the military and political role of a great power. A number of Italian historians, pointing out that the growth of big enterprises and, in general, of Italian capitalism were not, in 1915, minor achievements, see the roots of this considerable development in the choices made during the 1870s and 1880s. Their view can be summarized as follows:

> The thrust that protectionism gave to intellectual modernization was not, however, limited to the attention to the technical and scientific progress useful for production: it was more generally an impulse to react, in full harmony with the positivist climate, against the abstract, the codified, the dogmatic, in the name of a culture of 'things', explorations, experience.[39]

This argument, however, goes beyond the technical appraisal of economic policy to embrace far more general and important questions which go from the role of ideology in promoting development to the overall evaluation of the results achieved by the Italian economy after the War and to the causes of the authoritarian aftermath of Liberal Italy.

Development and the 'southern question'

Frequent reference has been made in this volume to countries which industrialize 'late' or are 'backward' with respect to those in which modern economic growth is well underway. The reference to 'countries' rather than to single regional areas has already been justified (see Chapter one), but geographical diffusion of growth does not respect national boundaries and regional economic imbalances characterize almost all the national cases of industrialization during the nineteenth century.

The gap in per capita income between north and south in Italy was particularly wide and difficult to eradicate: in 1988 GDP per capita in southern Italy was only 58 per cent that of the rest of the country; it may be said, therefore, that a 'southern question' is still open. The width and the persistence of 'dualism' were, therefore, the most characteristic traits of Italian modern economic growth, so much so that sometimes the southern question and development have been identified as a single problem: the Gramscian thesis is a case in point.

Two opinions can be advanced as to the origins of territorial imbalance.[40] The first comes immediately after the Unification and attributes to this and to Piedmontese policies the poverty of the south as compared to the rest of the country. If the more radical thesis of a colonialist exploitation of a prosperous south by the north, whose only merit was that of finding itself on the winning side in the Franco-Austrian war of 1859[41] has received little credit, the view of Nitti has been widely accepted. This line of thought holds that Unification was followed by a net transfer of resources from the south to the north through fiscal policy and the role of the banks.[42]

Diametrically opposed to Nitti's view is that of Fortunato in whose opinion 'everyone believed that the south was the promised land, overflowing with celestial gifts, not matched in energy by its inhabitants' while it was necessary to understand that this was a country 'that geography and history had for centuries condemned to poverty: economic poverty and moral poverty, the latter even sadder than the former, from which only political Unity, moved by the sentiment of common defence, could save it.'[43] Prevailing opinion today on this specific point seems closer to that of Fortunato, even though there has been no systematic quantitative study of the economic gap between north and south during the 1850s. On the other hand, many historians disagree with the view that 'one must recognize that the Unification did not fail to introduce immediately in the south considerable elements of economic progress.'[44]

However one considers the problem of origins, there remains that of the likely (though as yet unquantified) increase in the inter-regional economic gap after the Unification. Advocates of free trade have blamed economic policies: the creation of large firms with the help of tariffs and government orders, the duty on grain, railways, and the links established between large banks and heavy industry are seen as elements of a single way of promoting the country's growth, serving the interests of the north at the expense of those in the south. It matters little whether there was an explicit design to transfer resources from the less developed area to the richer one: the growth pattern that was followed inevitably implied a widening of the interregional gap. According to Salvemini's weekly magazine *L'Unità* and Einaudi's *Riforma Sociale*, economic policy *tout court* and that aiming specifically at improving conditions in the south were one and the same thing. From this point of view, important extraordinary intervention would not be necessary, it would be enough to adopt a fair taxation system, capitalize on the comparative advantages of the southern areas, create a suitable environment for the natural development of profitable investments which the local banks would be able to support adequately. This is the classic interpretation of the dualism which makes it one and the same thing as the characteristics of the mechanism of accumulation which are often blamed for the political disaster of Liberal Italy ending up in Fascist dictatorship.[45]

The structural causes of dualism have not been very thoroughly examined. It is to Cafagna's credit[46] that he highlights the uncomplementary features of the southern and northern markets, the latter belonging to the European periphery due to the high cost and unreliability of rail transport.[47] There are, however, more general causes for economic dualism. When modern economic growth takes place in a country already characterized by an income gap between two main areas, the effects of dynamic economies of scale and agglomeration, of processes of 'learning by doing', and of similar factors tend to widen that gap. Therefore, it does not seem very likely that the free play of market forces would have succeeded, at least in the period of time desired, in redressing the imbalance. The solution to the problem probably implies the adoption of special measures 'to increase the productivity of the weaker sections of the integrated economy':[48] however, it is not easy to say what such measures might have been in the historical context of Liberal Italy.

All the studies of the southern question suffer from an acute lack of quantification. The only important work existing is that of Vera Zamagni[49] who reconstructs, among other things, for 1911, estimates of regional income. Although everyone recognizes that the 'southern question' is a national question and although the works dedicated to it would fill an entire library, many of the economist's questions as to the size and causes of Italian economic dualism between the Unification and the First World War remain unanswered.

Modern economic growth of Liberal Italy: final results

Angus Maddison's estimates of the aggregate growth of sixteen capitalist countries between 1871 and 1981 shows how, on the whole, the recessive phases were relatively few and limited to the years following the two World Wars and the great crisis of the early 1930s.[50] In particular, the growth rates of income during the period 1860–95 of the economies considered by Maddison indicate that Italy's stagnation remains a notable exception for which a satisfactory explanation has yet to be given. According to the existing national accounting statistics, 'modern economic growth' began in

Italy only in the last decade of the nineteenth century. If this picture is correct, we are facing, and need to explain, the remarkable failure of a ruling class which was aware, at least from the 1850s on, of the importance and requirements of economic growth.[51] In doing so it will be difficult to avoid recourse to a category such as economic backwardness to which many variables, both social and political, are linked.

However, given the dearth of quantitative history of the period, the doubt may arise that the level of per capita income did not remain completely unchanged during the first thirty years after the Unification. The early results of Fenoaltea's research present a quite different picture of industrial history than the one traditionally given: only when this research is completed will it be possible to say whether this 'new' picture is valid or not. Other clues to the existence of a less static situation may, perhaps, be seen in the indicators of wealth already referred to.[52] When an accurate revision of national accounting statistics replaces the existing series one should not be very surprised if the picture of the first thirty years of Italian economic history after the Unification presents itself as less static than it appears today.

However one judges the backwardness of the country in 1861 and evaluates the characteristics of modern economic growth in Italy, the final results seem considerable. The country succeeded in making a gigantic industrial and organizational effort which, despite all its shortcomings, permitted the victorious conclusion of a conflict carried out more on economic than military terrain and allowed it to take a place among the Great Powers at Versailles. Is an economic system which obtains such success thriving? Not very, according to free-tradist tradition and part of Marxist thought, since Liberal Italy did not survive the First World War and found its own failure in the inability to resist dictatorship. The same presumed development factors, the great oligopolistic and protected industry which fed financial capital and stipulated villainous pacts with the landed interests are seen by some historians to be at the origins of fascism.

The history of post-Unification Italy already contained knotty problems which produced a profound contradiction between the formal character of institutions and the actual way they operated in the social and political concrete reality, and it was the very presence of these old problems, which the ruling class had left unresolved, that in the years after the War was to be determining in provoking the crisis of the Liberal state.[53]

In this view, the proof of the old deficiencies of the Italian bourgeoisie and, more generally, of the shortcomings of Liberal Italy's growth pattern would be found, *ex post*, in the fact that dictatorship was the political outcome of sixty years of social and economic history, unable to generate a sufficiently strong liberal democracy. This way of judging the 'final result' is shared, with various nuances, by many Italian historians. Its most radical formulation can be summarized by saying that if

> in terms of general theory and comparative analysis we must admit that authoritarianism and capitalistic maturity can live together very well, why do we not shout out – instead of whispering it – that Italian fascism did not arise from Italy's economic backwardness, nor from the heartstrings of a late agricultural and commercial feudalism, but from the heart of modern capitalism, representing the final landing place of a ruling class which, despite all its defects, succeeded in placing the needs and the aporia of industrialization in the foreground?[54]

While it is certainly true that economic development and political authoritarianism are anything but incompatible, and while it would be improper to judge the strength of the former on the basis of the latter, it does not follow that 'Fascism represented the final framework of a flow of modernization.'[55] Fascism has few and contradictory features of a 'developing dictatorship'. As I have shown elsewhere, the elements of backwardness remained deeply rooted in the economic structure of the country in spite of the tremendous progress made by Liberal Italy.[56] Many of the problems of the Italian economy between the two World Wars – and especially endemic unemployment and underemployment and their exceptionally high peak in the early 1930s – drew their origin from the low agricultural incomes on which half the population had to subsist and from the low productivity of many manufacturing industries. In short, Italy remained a relatively backward country in the European context despite the tremendous improvement in the standard of living of the masses that had taken place under Liberal governments and despite the widespread cohabitation of backward with modern industries. Even a possible and likely upward revision of the estimates of per capita income for the years immediately preceding the First World War would not significantly change the position of Italy as a 'tail-light', followed only by Japan, in the group of countries which began their own process of modern economic growth in the last century. A major catching-up process with the more advanced countries would take place only after the end of the Second World War.

Notes and references

Chapter one: Growth of product

1 As defined by S. Kuznets in *Modern Economic Growth*, New Haven: Yale University Press, 1966.
2 A. Toynbee, in his famous lectures, was perhaps the first scholar to use this term consistently to indicate the initial phase of modern economic growth (A. Toynbee, *Lectures on the Industrial Revolution*, London: Rivingtons, 1884).
3 'Take-off' is one of the five phases of growth singled out by W.W. Rostow in *The Stages of Economic Growth*, Cambridge: Cambridge University Press, 1960.
4 The 'big spurt' is one of the typical interpretative elements of European industrialization during the nineteenth century proposed by A. Gerschenkron in *Economic Backwardness in Historical Perspective*, Cambridge (Mass.): Belknap Press, 1962.
5 S. Kuznets, op. cit., p. 487.
6 ibid., p. 488.
7 ibid., p. 16.
8 S. Pollard, *Peaceful Conquest*, Oxford: Oxford University Press, 1981.
9 S. Kuznets, op cit., pp. 490–500.
10 ISTAT, 'Indagine statistica sullo sviluppo del reddito nazionale in Italia dal 1861 al 1956', *Annali di Statistica*, Series VIII, vol. 9, Rome, 1957.
11 The tables summarizing this work were compiled by P. Ercolani, 'Documentazione statistica di base', in G. Fuà (ed.) *Lo sviluppo economico in Italia*, Milano: Franco Angeli, 1969, vol. III, pp. 380–460.
12 An excellent summary of the theoretical problems implied in the comparison of aggregates of national accounting may be found in D. Usher, *The Measurement of Economic Growth*, Oxford: Basil Blackwell, 1980.
13 Given the enormous qualitative differences in the services of such goods, it is by no means simple to find a satisfactory way of comparing the welfare provided by a car, for example, with an equivalent in terms of horses and carriages, or that given by a radio compared with various other types of entertainment.

An economic history of Liberal Italy

14 Unless explicit reference is made to another source, all the estimates
which follow are those of P. Ercolani, op. cit. The differences between
these estimates and ISTAT's are explained in O. Vitali, 'La stima del
valore aggiunto a prezzi costanti per rami di attività', in G. Fuà,
op. cit., pp. 463–77 (especially pp. 474–7).
15 The population grew at an average annual rate of 0.7 per cent in 1861–
96 – the same growth rate as that of GDP.
16 The best estimates so far are those in O. Vitali, *Aspetti dello sviluppo
economico italiano alla luce della ricostruzione della popolazione
attiva*, Rome: Università di Roma, 1970.
17 A. Gerschenkron, 'Osservazioni sul saggio di sviluppo industriale in
Italia 1881–1913', in *Moneta e Credito*, 1956.
18 This index for the period 1861–1913 was constructed by Fenoaltea in
1967 for a doctoral thesis at Harvard but has been published only
recently in S. Fenoaltea, 'Italy', in P.K. O'Brien (ed.) *Railways and the
Economic Development of Western Europe*, London: Macmillan,
1983, pp. 49–120.
19 These are estimates based on Gerschenkron's indices (A. Gerschenkron,
op. cit.; and those of OECE, *Statistiques industrielles 1900–1959*,
Paris: OECE, 1960.

Chapter two: Demand

1 On law and order see J.A. Davis, *Conflict and Control – Law and
Order in Nineteenth-Century Italy*, London: Macmillan, 1988.
2 O. Vitali, 'La stima degli investimenti', in G. Fuà (ed.) *Lo sviluppo
economico in Italia*, Milan: Angeli, 1969, vol. III, pp. 478–537.
3 Cf. D. Usher, *The Measurement of Economic Growth*, Oxford: Basil
Blackwell, 1980.
4 S. Fenoaltea, 'Le opere pubbliche in Italia, 1861–1913', in *Rivista di
Storia Economica*, II (1985), pp. 335–69.
5 P. Ercolani, 'Documentazione statistica di base', in G. Fuà, op. cit.,
pp. 432–3.
6 In 1872 and 1878 there were very small trade surpluses.

Chapter three: The financial superstructure

1 See the essays in R. Cameron (ed.), *Banking and Economic Development*, Oxford: Oxford University Press, 1972.
2 R.W. Goldsmith, *Financial Structure and Development*, New Haven
and London: Yale University Press, 1969.
3 R.W. Goldsmith, op. cit., p. 27.
4 ibid., p. 41.
5 R. De Mattia (ed.), *I bilanci degli Istituti di emissione italiani (1845–
1936)*, Rome: Banca d'Italia, 1967.
6 A.M. Biscaini Cotula and P.L. Ciocca, 'Le strutture finanziarie:

152

aspetti quantitativi di lungo periodo (1870–1979)', in F. Vicarelli (ed.), *Capitale industriale e capitale finanziario: il caso italiano*, Bologna: Il Mulino, 1979, pp. 61–136.
7 United Kingdom, United States, France, Japan, and Germany.
8 Income elasticity of the financial intermediaries' liabilities was 1.25 in 1896–1913 and 3.0 in 1887–96.
9 A.M. Biscaini Cotula and P.L. Ciocca, op. cit., p. 67.
10 ibid.

Chapter four: Production, productivity, and welfare

1 See D. Usher, *The Measurement of Economic Growth*, Oxford: Basil Blackwell, 1980.
2 S. Kuznets, *Modern Economic Growth*, New Haven: Yale University Press, 1966, p. 491.
3 ibid., p. 9.
4 ibid., p. 73.
5 O. Vitali, *Aspetti dello sviluppo economico italiano alla luce della ricostruzione della popolazione attiva*, Rome: Università di Roma, 1970.
6 G. Fuà, *Formazione, distribuzione e impiego del reddito dal 1861: sintesi statistica*, Rome: ISCO, 1972, Tables 2.9 et seq.
7 G. Fuà, op. cit., Table 2.6.
8 See P.K. O'Brien and G. Toniolo, 'Sull'arretratezza dell'agricoltura italiana rispetto a quella del Regno Unito attorno al 1910', in *Ricerche Economiche*, 1987, pp. 266–85; and G. Toniolo and F. Piva, 'Unemployment in the Nineteenthirties: the Case of Italy', in B. Eichengreen and T. Hutton (eds), *Interwar Unemployment in International Perspective*, Ondrech, Boston, and London: Kluwer, 1988, pp. 221–46.
9 In his comparative work Vitali ignored the first two censuses because the data were too unreliable for a reconstruction of the labour force.
10 G. Fuà. op. cit., Table 5.3.
11 ibid., Tables 5.20 and 5.21.
12 N.F.R. Crafts, 'New Estimates of GNP in Europe', in *Explorations in Economic History*, XX (1983), p. 389.
13 B. Barbieri, *I consumi nel primo secolo dell'Unità d'Italia, 1861–1960*, Milan: Giuffré, 1961, p. 24, with corrections by P. Sabbatucci Severini and G. Toniolo, 'Aspetti macroeconomici del problema della povertà in Italia', in *Ricerche di storia sociale e religiosa*, X (1981), p. 22.
14 Taking 100 as the average availability of meat per head in Italy, that of other countries is as follows: England 228; France 182; Switzerland 178; Austria 155; Germany and the Low Countries 140. (Estimates by Sabbatucci Severini and Toniolo, op. cit., p. 31 from B.R. Mitchell, *European Historical Statistics 1750–1970*, London: Macmillan, 1975).
15 Assuming an average per capita consumption of 45 kilogrammes of meat for the 20 per cent of the population resident in large urban

centres, the remaining 80 per cent only had 9 kilogrammes per head per annum.

16 S. Somogyi, 'L'alimentazione nell'Italia unita', in *Storia d'Italia*, Turin: Einaudi, 1975, vol. V, book I, p. 852.

17 ibid., p. 851.

18 ISTAT, *Sommario di statistiche storiche*, Rome, 1969, p. 27. The data are averages for the periods 1881–2 and 1899–1902 respectively. In 1900 life expectancy (in years) at birth was: Sweden 55.7; United Kingdom 50.7; USA 47.3; France 47.0; Germany 46.6; Austria 40.1 (cf. A. Maddison *Phases of Capitalist Development*, Oxford: Oxford University Press, 1982, p. 189).

19 ISTAT, op. cit., p. 22.

Chapter five: Before the Unification

1 A. Caracciolo, 'La storia economica', in *Storia d'Italia*, Turin, Einaudi, 1976, vol. III, p. 517.

2 C.M. Cipolla, *Four Centuries of Italian Demographic Development*, in V. Glass and C. Eversley, *Population in History*, London, 1965, pp. 570–87.

3 B.R. Mitchell, *European Historical Statistics 1750–1970*, London: Macmillan, 1975, p. 5. In the first case the growth from 1700–70 was 0.38 per cent per annum, in the second only 0.2 per cent.

4 ibid. The growth rates would be as follows: 1770–1800: 0.53 per cent, 1800–25: 0.52 per cent, 1825–48: 0.79 per cent.

5 A. Caracciolo, op. cit., p. 518.

6 ibid.

7 ibid., pp. 520–3.

8 See, for example, P. Mathias, *The First Industrial Nation*, London: Methuen, 1983.

9 P. Bairoch, 'Europe's Gross National Product: 1800–1975', in *The Journal of European Economic History*, vol. V, 1976, p. 286.

10 Among other things, one must consider the slow rate at which British per capita income grew, until 1780, in the context of a strong demographic increase. Even between 1780 and 1800 it grew by only 1 per cent per annum.

11 After a brief 'reawakening' during the fifteenth century, feudalism had once again declined. However, even in the eighteenth century there were still large imperial feudal domains, and while these often differed greatly from region to region, the areas in which the ancient feudal privileges were most jealously guarded were in the Republic of Venice and in the Kingdom of Sardinia.

12 P. Villani, *Mezzogiorno tra riforme e rivoluzione*, Bari: Laterza, 1973, p. 155.

13 ibid., p. 164.

14 ibid., p. 200.

15 See L. De Rosa, 'Property Rights, Institutional Change and Economic

Growth in Southern Italy', in *The Journal of European Economic History*, vol. VIII, 1979, pp. 543–45.

16 A. Caracciolo, op. cit., p. 561.

17 For further details see G. Sotgiu, *Storia della Sardegna sabauda*, Bari: Laterza, 1984.

18 R. Romeo, *Dal Piemonte sabaudo all'Italia liberale*, Torino: Einaudi, 1963, p. 127.

19 See the volumes of the 'Archivio Economico dell'Unificazione Italiana' commissioned by Pasquale Saraceno for the twenty-fifth anniversary of the foundation of IRI, edited by Carlo Maria Cipolla.

20 P. Bairoch, op. cit., p. 286.

21 G. Porisini, 'Produttività e agricoltura: i rendimenti del frumento in Italia dal 1815 al 1922', in *Archivio Economico dell'Unificazione Italiana*, Turin, ILTE, 1971, p. 16.

22 M. Romani, *Storia economica d'Italia nel secolo XIX*, Bologna: Il Mulino, 1982, pp. 154–5.

23 ibid., p. 157. Given Italy's oligopolistic position in this sector, prices doubled, but production costs grew likewise owing to the fall in unit yields and the necessity to import silkworm eggs at high and increasing prices.

24 L. Cafagna, *Intorno alle origini del dualismo economico italiano*, in A. Caracciolo (ed.), *Problemi storici dell'industrializzazione e dello sviluppo*, Urbino: Argalia, 1969, p. 120.

25 A. Caracciolo, op. cit., pp. 619–20.

26 ibid.

27 L. Cafagna, 'The Industrial Revolution in Italy 1830–1914', in C.M. Cipolla (ed.), *The Fontana Economic History of Europe*, vol. IV, Glasgow: Fontana-Collins, 1973, p. 280.

28 'For some hundred years, from the Restoration to the First World War, silk led the field in Italian exports, more or less regularly representing about a third of their total value.' Ibid., p. 281.

29 A. Caracciolo, op. cit., p. 630.

30 R. Romeo, *Breve storia della grande industria in Italia*, Bologna: Capelli, 1972, p. 20.

31 M. Romani, op. cit., pp. 396–7.

32 A. Caracciolo, op. cit., p. 622.

33 Production of pig-iron (in thousands of tonnes)

	1850	1860
United Kingdom	2285	3888
France	406	898
Germany	210	529
Russia	228	298

Source: B.R. Mitchell, op. cit., pp. 215–16.

34 M. Merger, 'Un modello di sostituzione: la locomotiva italiana dal 1850 al 1914', in *Rivista di Storia Economica*, vol. III, 1986, pp. 66–108.
35 A. Caracciolo, *Stato e società civile*, Turin: Einaudi, 1960, p. 22.
36 A. Caracciolo, 'La storia economica', p. 691.
37 ibid., pp. 572–7, and J. Davis, *Società e imprenditori nel regno borbonico 1815–1860*, Bari: Laterza, 1979.
38 See A. Graziani, 'Il commercio estero del Regno delle Due Sicillie' in *Archivio Economico dell'Unificazione Italiana*, vol. X, Rome, 1960, pp. 9–10.
39 ibid., p. 10. More important still was the Trade and Navigation Treaty signed with the United Kingdom in April, 1945 (M. Romani, op. cit., p. 86).
40 A. Caracciolo, 'La storia economica', pp. 608 *et seq.*
41 G. Parenti, 'Il commercio estero del Granducato di Toscana dal 1851 al 1859', in *Archivio Economico dell'Unificazione Italiana*, series I, vol. VIII, Rome 1959, p. 20.
42 I. Glazier, 'Il commercio estero del Regno Lombardo-Veneto dal 1815 al 1865', in *Archivio Economico dell'Unificazione Italiana*, series I, vol. XV, Rome, 1966. For Austrian Customs policy see J. Komlos, *The Habsburg Monarchy as a Customs Union*, Princeton: Princeton University Press, 1983.
43 F. Bonelli, 'Il commercio estero dello stato pontificio nel secolo XIX', in *Archivio Economico dell'Unificazione Italiana*, series I, vol. XI, Rome, 1961, pp. 43 *et seq.*
44 See R. Romeo, *Vita di Cavour*, Bari: Laterza, 1984, pp. 192 *et seq.*
45 G. Felloni, 'Le entrate degli stati sabaudi dal 1825 al 1860', in *Archivio Economico dell'Unificazione Italiana*, vols. III–IV, Rome, 1956 and 'Le spese effettive e il bilancio degli stati sabaudi dal 1825 al 1869', in *Archivio Economico dell'Unificazione Italiana*, vol. IX, Rome 1956. In 1849 the deficit was 132 per cent of total revenue and it fell to 12 per cent in the course of the decade.
46 R. Romeo, *Vita di Cavour*, p. 202.
47 ibid., p. 201.
48 R. Romeo, *Cavour e il suo tempo*, vol. II, Bari Laterza, 1977, pp. 682–3.

Chapter six: Economic problems of the Unification

1 G. Carocci, *Storia d'Italia dall'Unità a oggi*, Milano: Feltrinelli, 1975, p. 18.
2 ibid., p. 19.
3 E. Ragionieri, 'La storia politica e sociale' in *Storia d'Italia*, Turin: Einaudi, 1976, vol. IV, p. 1674.
4 In 1861 the Kingdom of Italy had around 22 million subjects. Only the Russian and Habsburg Empires, and France had larger populations. In 1871 the German Reich had a population of 41 million. The inhabitants

of the United Kingdom, including Ireland, were 29 million: 2 million more than Italy had after the conquest of the Veneto and Lazio, according to the 1871 census. Spain, in 1861, had only 15.6 million inhabitants. None of the other European states had more than 10 million (Cf. B.R. Mitchell, *European Historical Statistics 1750–1970*, London: Macmillan, 1975, pp. 3 *et seq.*).

5 I. Chabod, 'Considerazioni sulla politica estera dell'Italia dal 1870 al 1915', in *Orientamenti per la storia italiana del Risorgimento*, Bari: Laterza, 1952, p. 25.

6 According to Kuznets' estimates, given Italy's per capita income as 100 in this period, the index for the other countries was as follows: United Kingdom 230, Switzerland 200, The Netherlands and Belgium 180 (S. Kuznets, *Economic Growth of Nations. Total Output and Production Structure*, Cambridge, Mass.: Belknap, 1971, p. 24). In Bairoch's estimates (P. Bairoch, 'Europe's Gross National Product 1800–1975' in *The Journal of European Economic History*, vol. V. 1976) the gap, though smaller, is none the less considerable: United Kingdom 194, Switzerland 160, Belguim 163, Netherlands 150.

7 B.R. Mitchell, op. cit., pp. 251 *et seq.*

8 ibid., pp. 211 *et seq.*

9 A rough indicator of the railways' importance is given by tonnes transported per kilometres of track. The index would be as follows (1871): Great Britain 7,800; Austria-Hungary 4,200; Belgium 3,800; France 2,400; Italy and Spain 800.

10 A. Caracciolo, 'La storia economica' in *Storia d'Italia*, Turin: Einaudi, 1976.

11 G. Luzzatto, *L'economia italiana dal 1861 al 1914*, Milano: Banca Commerciale Italiana, 1963, p. 19.

12 A. Caracciolo, op. cit., p. 680.

13 G. Porisini, 'Produttività e agricoltura: i rendimenti del frumento in Italia dal 1815 al 1922', in *Archivio Economico dell'Unificazione Italiana*, Turin: ILTE, 1971, p. 16.

14 M. Aymard, 'Rendements et productivité agricole dans l'Italie moderne', in *Annales*, XXVIII (1973), p. 497. It had not escaped the notice of the early nineteenth century Neapolitan economists that cereal cultivation in the south was at odds with the comparative advantages of an area with a high concentration of labour and a climate suitable for high-quality crops. See, for example: D. Balsamo, *Memorie economiche e agrarie riguardanti il Regno di Sicilia*, Palermo, Reale Stamperia, 1803 and N. Palmieri, *Saggio sulle cause e i rimedi delle angustie attuali dell'economia agraria in Sicilia*, Palermo, Reale Stamperia, 1826.

15 Only 57.2 per cent of those entitled to vote did so (Cf. R. Romeo, *Vita di Cavour*, Bari: Laterza, 1984, p. 508).

16 G. Candeloro, *Storia dell'Italia moderna*, vol. IV, Milan: Feltrinelli, 1980, p. 534.

17 Segretariato Generale della Camera dei Deputati, *Il Parlamento dell'Unità d'Italia (1859–61)*, vol. II, Rome, 1961, p. 55.

18 ibid., vol. III, pp. 8–9.
19 E. Ragionieri, 'La storia politica e sociale', p. 1685.
20 Cf. E. Ragionieri, *Politica e amministrazione nella storia dell'Italia Unità*, Bari: Laterza, 1967, p. 104.
21 See A. Caracciolo, *Stato e società civile*, Turin, Einaudi, 1960, p. 22.
22 E. Ragionieri, 'La storia politica e sociale', p. 1685.
23 R. Romeo, op. cit., p. 496.
24 ibid., p. 497.
25 R. Romeo, op. cit., p. 195.
26 M. Romani, *Storia economica d'Italia nel secolo XIX*, Bologna: Il Mulino, 1982, p. 206.
27 A. Plebano, *Storia della finanza italiana*, Turin: Frassati, 1899, vol. I, p. 76.
28 My estimates based on the data of P. Maestri, *L'Italia economica nel 1868*, Florence: Civelli, 1869, pp. 323–4.
29 Q. Sella quoted in A. Plebano, op. cit., p. 114.
30 Gold was valued at 3.437 lire per gramme and silver at 0.2205 lire per gramme (E. Corbino, *Annali dell'economia italiana*, Milan: IPSOA, 1981, vol, I, p. 281).
31 In 1866 the monetary convention was ratified between Italy, France, Belgium and Switzerland (whose currencies all had the same intrinsic value and, therefore, a rate of exchange of one to one).
32 Note the limiting use of *in the* (*nel*) instead of *of the* (*del*) which would have indicated, if nothing else, a supremacy equal to that of the Bank *of* England and of the Banque *de* France.
33 G. Luzzatto, op. cit., pp. 63–4. On an important aspect of monetary unification see V. Sannucci, 'The establishment of a central bank in Italy in the 19th century' and comments by C. Goodhart and G. Toniolo in M. de Cecco and A. Giovannini (eds) *A European Central Bank?*, Cambridge: Cambridge University Press, 1989, pp. 244–89.

Chapter seven: The age of the Right

1 R. Romeo, *Risorgimento e capitalismo*, Bari: Laterza, 1959, p. 111.
2 For the period in question (1861–76) ISTAT–Fuà and Fenoaltea give the same growth rate (cf. Table 2.3).
3 ISTAT, 'Indagine statistica sullo sviluppo del reddito nazionale in Italia dal 1861 al 1856', in *Annali di Statistica*, Series VIII, Rome, 1957.
4 In his calculation of total production, Romeo uses data relative 'to the frontiers of the time . . . to make these calculations compare with those of Bodio' (*Risorgimento e capitalismo*, Bari: Laterza, 1959, p. 111). In this way he obtains an average annual growth of 2.0 per cent between 1861–3 and 1875–7. This growth would be very similar to that achieved during the Giolitti years. However, the population increased in the same period by 1.5 per cent each year. The increase in both production and population was clearly the result of the conquest of the Veneto (1866) and of Lazio (1870), as the small per capita increase

shows. A similar result may be obtained taking the period 1861–80 considered by Romeo. A very different result is obtained, however, by using Bodio's data. Taking into account the increase in agricultural prices, the growth rate of production in that sector is 1.1 per cent a year, *per capita*, from 1862–80.

5 For the amount of outstanding debt see E. Corbino, *Annali dell'economia italiana (1861–1870)*, Milan: IPSOA, 1982, vol. I.
6 ibid., p. 281.
7 G. Luzzatto, *L'economia italiana dal 1861 al 1914*, Milan: Banca Commerciale Italiana, 1963.
8 This with respect to gold standard currencies.
9 Average premium and discount values. (E. Corbino, op. cit., vol. I).
10 ISTAT, *Sommario di statistiche storiche*, Rome, 1969, p. 172.
11 A. Confalonieri, *Banca e industria in Italia 1894–1906*, Milan: Banca Commerciale Italiana, 1974.
12 S. Fenoaltea, 'Italy', in P.K. O'Brien (ed.), *Railways and Economic Development 1830–1914*, London: Macmillan, 1983, p. 52. The extension of the network was as follows: Great Britain 15,000 km, Germany 12,000 km, France 9,000 km, Spain and Italy 2,000 km. The index of kilometres of rail per square kilometre was as follows: Great Britain 100, Germany 34, France 26, Italy 11, Spain 6.
13 E. Corbino, op. cit., p. 182.
14 For the most recent estimates see S. Fenoaltea, 'Le costruzioni in Italia', in *Rivista di Storia Economica*, I (1984), pp. 61–94.
15 S. Fenoaltea, 'Le opere pubbliche in Italia, 1861–1913', in *Rivista di Storia Economica*, II (1985).
16 For a clear summary of the problems faced and the methods used to solve them see: P.K. O'Brien, *The New Economic History of the Railways*, London: Croom Helm, 1977.
17 Cf. 'Atti della commissione d'inchiesta sull'esercizio delle ferrovie', Rome, 1881. The inquiry paved the way for the 1885 Act discussed in the following chapter.
18 B. Caizzi, *Il commercio*, Turin: Utet, 1975, p. 78.
19 'The 1865 Railway Act made provision for a subsidy per kilometre and, in some cases, guaranteed a minimum yield for railway shares. However, these subsidies often had to be raised – especially on lines operating in the South.' Fenoaltea estimates the internal rate of return on capital invested in railways in the mid-1870s to have been about 3 per cent. S. Fenoaltea, op. cit., p. 90.
20 ibid., pp. 81–2.
21 ibid., p. 86.
22 On this point cf. G. Toniolo, 'Railways and economic growth in Mediterranean countries: some methodological remarks', in P.K. O'Brien (ed.) op. cit., pp. 227–36.
23 S. Fenoaltea, 'Le ferrovie e lo sviluppo industriale italiano', in G. Toniolo, *L'economia italiana 1861–1940*, Bari: Laterza, 1978.
24 V. Castronovo, 'La storia economica', in *Storia d'Italia*, Turin, Einaudi, 1975, vol. IV (1), pp. 1–506.

25 R. Romeo, *Breve storia della grande industria in Italia*, Bologna, Cappelli, 1972, p. 41.
26 ISTAT, op. cit., p. 128.
27 ibid., p. 42.
28 R. Romano, *Borghesia industriale in ascesa*, Milan: Angeli, 1977.
29 R. Romano, *I Crespi*, Milan: Angeli, 1985, pp. 21–36.
30 Data on the importation of 'Cotone in massa greggia', in ISTAT, op. cit., p. 159.
31 B.R. Mitchell, *European Historical Statistics 1750–1970*, London: Macmillan, 1975, p. 258.
32 One need only mention the Rossi wool firm of Schio and the Manifattura Lane di Borgosesia which both became joint stock companies.
33 V. Castronovo, *L'industria italiana dall'ottocento a oggi*, Milan: Mondadori, 1980, p. 26.
34 ISTAT, op. cit., p. 159.
35 R. Romeo, *Breve storia*, pp. 45–6.
36 From 1862–75 the average annual increase in tonnage of ships launched was 10.1 per cent. After 1875, however, production fell rapidly and drastically and it was only in 1919 that production again exceeded that level. The greater average tonnage for that year (92,900 tonnes) indicates how much technological progress had been made by the Italian shipbuilding industry (data source: ISTAT, op. cit., p. 130).
37 M. Merger, 'Un modello di sostituzione: la locomotiva italiana dal 1850 al 1914', in *Rivista di Storia Economica*, III (1986), pp. 66–108.
38 V. Castronovo, *L'industria italiana*, p. 36.
39 See G. Carocci, *Storia d'Italia dall'Unità a oggi*, Milan, Feltrinelli, 1975, pp. 37–44.
40 For an idea of Sella's work and ideology see: G. Are, *Alle origini dell'Italia industriale*, Naples: Guida, 1974, p. 167.
41 G. Carocci, op. cit., p. 42.
42 G. De Rosa, *Storia del movimento cattolico in Italia dalla Restaurazione all'Età Giolittiana*, Bari: Laterza, 1966, p. 126.
43 G. Are, op. cit., p. 9.

Chapter eight: The contradictions of the 1880s

1 Given below are the average annual growth rates for industrial production in some countries from 1873–96. The years or periods when production fell are shown in brackets:

France 1.7 (1877, 1879, 1883–5, 1890, 1893, 1895).
Germany 2.9 (1880).
Russia 6.0 (1884, 1888).
Sweden 4.5 (1878, 1883, 1886, 1895).
United Kingdom 2.0 (1877–9, 1884–6, 1892–3).

Source: B.R. Mitchell, *European Historical Statistics 1850–1970*, London: Macmillan, 1975, p. 179.

2 Quantities and prices from ISTAT, *Sommario di statistiche storiche*, Rome, 1969, p. 106 and p. 172.

3 G. Porosini, 'Produttività e agricoltura: i rendimenti del frumento in Italia dal 1815 al 1922', *Archivio Economico dell'Unificazione Italiana*, Turin: ILTE, 1971.

4 ibid., p. 38. The same thesis is also held by E. Sereni, *Il capitalismo nelle campagne (1850–1900)*, Turin: Einaudi, 1968.

5 Taking the average production for 1875–7 as 100, that for 1885–8 was as follows: wheat 84.5, potatoes 104.5, oranges 126.0, wine 139.1, olive oil 75.3 (ISTAT, op. cit., pp. 106–12).

6 G. Federico, 'Commercio dei cereali e dazio sul grano in Italia (1863–1913). Un'analisi quantitativa', in *Nuova Rivista Storica*, LXVIII (1984), pp. 46–108.

7 The fall, between 1875–87 and 1886–8, exceeded 8 per cent according to the data of B. Barbieri in *I consumi nel primo secolo dell'unità d'Italia 1861–1960*, Milan: Giuffré, 1961, p. 129.

8 G. Orlando, *Storia della politica agraria in Italia dal 1848 a oggi*, Bari: Laterza, 1984, p. 40.

9 ibid., p. 42.

10 A. Gerschenkron, *Economic Backwardness in Historical Perspective*, Cambridge, Mass.: Belknap Press, 1962, p. 386.

11 Cf. F. Bonelli, *Lo sviluppo di una grande impresa in Italia. La Terni dal 1884 al 1962*, Turin: Einaudi, 1975.

12 ISTAT, op. cit., p. 28.

13 ibid.

14 In 1889 the Breda works already produced forty-nine locomotives. (See M. Merger, 'Un modello di sostituzione: la locomotiva italiana dal 1850 al 1914', *Rivista di Storia Economica*, III (1986), pp. 66–108).

15 ibid.

16 E. Corbino, *Annali dell'economia italiana (1871–1880)*, Milan: IPSOA, 1982, vol. II, p. 117.

17 M. Warglien, 'Nota sull'investimento industriale in macchinari e altre attrezzature meccaniche: Italia 1881–1913', in *Rivista di Storia Economica*, II (1985), p. 125.

18 E. Corbino, op. cit.

19 One notable exception was, perhaps, the Cassa di Risparmio delle Province Lombarde, which even then was fairly large and operated on a regional level.

20 A. Confalonieri, *Banca e industria in Italia 1894–1906*, Milan: Banca Commerciale Italiana, 1974, vol. I, p. 276.

21 ibid., p. 273.

22 ibid.

23 Note, for example, the commitment of the Banca Popolare di Vicenza to the local tram company. Because of that the Bank was involved in a serious crisis shortly before the First World War.

24 A. Confalonieri, op. cit., p. 284.

25 M. Warglien, 'Investimento industriale e instabilità finanziaria in

Italia, 1878–1913', in *Rivista di Storia Economica*, III (1987), pp. 384–439.

26 ibid.

27 G. Candeloro, *Storia dell'Italia moderna*, Milan: Feltrinelli, 1980, vol. VI, p. 248.

28 S. Fenoaltea, 'Italy', in P.K. O'Brien (ed.) *Railways and the Economic Development of Western Europe*, London: Macmillan, 1983, pp. 92–4.

29 ibid.

30 During his first Prime Ministership, Depretis himself was also Finance Minister. During the second and third Depretis governments (December 1877, March 1878, July 1879) (Magliani held this post, and continued to do so successively without interruption from Cairoli's third government (November 1879–May 1881) until 29 December 1888.

31 In 1877 direct taxation was reformed. In 1884 the unpopular tax on milled grain was abolished (but local duties on flour remained). The Land Register Act (Cadastre) was passed in 1886 and land tax was reformed.

32 In February of that year the measure was passed in the Lower Chamber with only 27 votes against out of 293 voting members.

33 Corbino's criticisms of this operation are interesting especially considering the period in which they were made (E. Corbino, *Annali dell' economia italiana (1881–1890)*, Milan: IPSOA, 1982, vol. III, p. 332).

34 M. Minghetti, *Discorsi Parlamentari, Camera dei Deputati*, Rome, 1890, vol. VIII, p. 89.

35 The average devaluation of the lira with respect to currencies convertible into gold was 10.5 per cent in 1880 and 9.5 per cent from 1875 to 1880 (Cf. E. Corbino, op. cit., vol. III, p. 318).

36 After 1884 the fall in French prices was, however, more rapid and longer-lasting than in Italy's; this explains some of the reasons for the trade war of 1887–8.

37 G. Carocci, *Storia d'Italia dall'Unità a oggi*, Milan: Feltrinelli, 1975, pp. 46–7.

38 The Tariff Act was passed on 30 May and came into force on 1 July 1878.

39 The 1886 'fiscal duty' was raised to 1.4 lire per quintal in 1883.

40 G. Federico, op. cit., p. 105.

41 To these treaties should be added the extension of those already signed with Great Britain, Germany, Switzerland and Belgium, as well as the operating of the 'most-favoured nation' clause.

42 S. Lanaro, *Nazione e lavoro*, Venice: Marsilio, 1979, p. 170.

43 The Act was approved by a large majority (199 for and 27 against) on 14 July 1887. Ironically, this was to be one of the last actions of the free-trader Depretis' government since he died two weeks later (29 July). The new tariff came into force on 1 January 1888.

44 There were further increases in 1893 (seven lire per quintal) and in late 1894 (7.5 lire per quintal).

45 Though very rough-and-ready calculations they are probably not far from the truth.

46 G. Toniolo, 'Effective Protection and Industrial Growth: the Case of Italian Engineering 1896–1913', in *The Journal of European Economic History*, V (1977), pp. 659–73.

Chapter nine: A decade of crisis 1887–96

1 G. Luzzato, *L'economia italiana dal 1861 al 1914*, Milan: Banca Commerciale Italiana, 1963, vol. I, p. 251.
2 A good account of the intertwining of the economic and political crises can be found in G. Manacorda, *Crisi economica e lotta politica in Italia, 1892–1896*, Turin: Einaudi, 1968.
3 G. Candeloro, *Storia dell'Italia moderna*, Milan: Feltrinelli, 1980, vol. VI, p. 329.
4 'There is no doubt that Parliament and government were strongly lobbied by outside groups' (G. Luzzatto, op. cit., p. 227).
5 For a contemporary view see B. Stringher, 'Il commercio con l'estero e il corso dei cambi', in *La Nuova Antologia*, 1814, pp. 15–23. Among the historians, see especially G. Luzzatto, op. cit. and A. Confalonieri, *Banca e industria in Italia 1894–1906*, Milan: Banca Commerciale Italiana, 1974, vol. I.
6 M. Warglien, 'Investimento industriale e instabilità finanziaria in Italia (1878–1913)', in *Rivista di Storia Economica*, III (1987), pp. 384–439.
7 ibid., p. 19 and Fig. II.
8 G. Luzzatto, op. cit., p. 244.
9 ibid., p. 247.
10 M. Warglien, 'Nota sull'investimento industriale in macchinari e altre attrezzature meccaniche: Italia 1881–1913', in *Rivista di Storia Economica*, II (1985), pp. 125–46.
11 F. Bonelli, *La Terni: lo sviluppo di una grande impresa*, Turin: Einaudi, 1975.
12 G. Luzzatto, op. cit., p. 247.
13 M. Pantaleoni, 'La caduta della Società Generale di Credito Mobiliare Italiano', in *Il Giornale dagli Economisti*, 1895.
14 G. Luzzatto, op. cit., p. 251.
15 ibid., p. 253.
16 ibid.
17 G. Di Nardi, *Le banche di emissione in Italia nel secolo XIX*, Turin: UTET, 1954.
18 E. Vitale, *La riforma degli Istituti di emissione e gli 'scandali bancari' in Italia, 1892–96*, Rome: Camera dei Deputati, 1972, vol. I, p. 12.
19 G. Candeloro, op. cit., vol. VI, p. 426.
20 I am indebted to Sergio Cardarelli for this and other information taken from the Minutes of the Consiglio Superiore della Banca Nazionale nel Regno.
21 See M. Panateleoni, in *The Economist*, 1894.
22 Regio Decreto 21/2/1894, no. 5, art. 2.

23 G. Manacorda, op. cit., p. 187.
24 ibid., p. 175.
25 E. Corbino, *Annali dell'economia italiana (1891–1900)*, Milan: IPSOA, 1982, vol. IV, p. 319.
26 Banca d'Italia, 'Verbali del Consiglio Superiore', Session of 6 January 1895, pp. 14–15.

Chapter ten: The Age of Giolitti

1 J.M. Keynes, *The Economic Consequences of the Peace*, London: Macmillan, 1920, p. 9.
2 S. Fenoaltea, 'Edilizia e opere pubbliche in Italia', in *Rivista di Storia Economica*, IV (1987).
3 M. Warglien, 'Nota sull'investimento industriale in macchinari e altre attrezzature meccaniche: Italia 1881–1913', in *Rivista di Storia Economica*, II (1985), p. 145.
4 G. Fuà (ed.), *Lo sviluppo economico in Italia*, Milan: Franco Angeli, 1969, vol. I.
5 V. Zamagni, 'I salari giornalieri degli operai dell'industria nell'età giolittiana', in *Rivista di Storia Economica*, I (1984), p. 195.
6 In 1899 exports exceeded imports by 16 per cent.
7 B. King, 'Statistics of Italy', in *Journal of the Royal Statistical Society*, LXVI (1903), pp. 242–44.
8 P.K. O'Brien and G. Toniolo, 'Sull'arretratezza dell'agricoltura italiana rispetto a quello del Regno Unito attorno al 1910', in *Richerche Economiche*, 1987, pp. 266–85.
9 In particular, the production of meat and wine is probably underestimated. (G. Federico, 'Per una valutazione delle statistiche della produzione agricola italiana dopo l'unità (1861–1913)', in *Società e Storia*, 1982, p. 118).
10 G. Federico, 'Commercio dei cereali e dazio sul grano in Italia (1863–1913). Un'analisi quantitativa', in *Nuova Rivista Storica*, LXVIII (1984).
11 The French and German duties were 6.5 and 7 lire per quintal respectively (G. Orlando, *Storia della politica agraria in Italia dal 1848 a oggi*, Bari: Laterza, 1984, p. 73).
12 G. Federico, 'Commercio dei cereali', p. 77.
13 The duty on sugar was doubled (fom 50 to 99 lire per quintal) in 1894.
14 G. Orlando, op. cit., p. 88.
15 ibid., p. 77.
16 B. Stringher, *Notizie sull'Italia agricola*, Rome: Bertero, 1905, pp. 18 *et seq*.
17 G. Orlando, op. cit., p. 75.
18 On this subject see the very clear opinion of Gerschenkron (in *Economic Backwardness in Historial Perspective*, Cambridge, Mass.: Belknap Press, 1962) and those expressed in some of the essays in A. Caracciolo (ed.), *La formazione dell'Italia industriale*, Bari: Laterza, 1969.

19 See, even though the tone and motivation are different: A. Gerschenkron, op. cit.; S. Fenoaltea, 'Riflessioni sull'esperienza industriale italiana dal Risorgimento alla prima guerra mondiale', in G. Toniolo (ed.), *L'economia italiana 1861–1940*, Bari: Laterza, 1978; V. Castronovo, *L'industria italiana dall'ottocento a oggi*, Milan: Mondadori, 1980.

20 P. Ercolani, 'Documentazione statistica di base', in G. Fuà (ed.), op. cit., p. 411.

21 V. Castronovo, op. cit., p. 96.

22 E. Corbino, *Annali dell'economia italiana (1901–1914)*, Milan: IPSOA, 1982, vol. V, p. 138.

23 O. Vitali, *Aspetti dello sviluppo economico italiano alla luce della ricostruzione della popolazione attiva*, Rome: Ateneo, 1970, pp. 337–43.

24 P.K. O'Brien and G. Toniolo, op. cit.

25 V. Zamagni, op. cit., pp. 183–208.

26 L. Favero and G. Tassello, 'Cent'anni di emigrazione italiana', in G. Rosoli (ed.), *Un secolo di emigrazione italiana: 1876–1976*, Rome: Centro studi emigrazione, 1976, p. 21.

27 ibid., pp. 25–30.

28 A. Confalonieri, *Banca e industria in Italia*, Milan: Banca Commerciale Italiana, 1975, vol. II, pp. 32 *et seq*.

29 See Chapter twelve, part 3. For a summary of this view of the role of the banks see also: J.S. Cohen, 'Italy', in R. Cameron (ed.) *Banking and Economic Development*, Oxford: Oxford University Press, 1972.

30 A. Confalonieri, op. cit., vol. III, 1976, p. 459.

31 P. Ciocca and G. Toniolo, 'Industry and Finance in Italy 1918–1940', in *The Journal of European Economic History*, 13 (1984), Special Issue, pp. 113–37.

32 F. Bonelli, *La crisi del 1907*, Turin, Fondazione Einaudi, 1971, p. 29 *et seq*.

33 The two 'German' banks rapidly became Italianized, but this fact was always denied by their enemies who used it against them especially during the First World War.

34 F. Bonelli, op. cit., p. 94.

35 ibid., p. 124.

36 ibid., pp. 156–7.

37 ibid., p. 158.

38 ibid., p. 164.

39 A. Confalonieri, *Banca e industria in Italia dalla crisi del 1907 all'agosto 1914*, Milan: Banca Commerciale Italiana, 1982, p. 519.

40 G. Carocci, *Storia d'Italia dall'Unità ad oggi*, Milan: Feltrinelli, 1975, pp. 135–6.

41 E. Corbino, op. cit., pp. 191 *et seq*.

42 G. Toniolo, 'Effective Protection and Industrial Growth: The Case of Italian Engineering, 1898–1913', in *The Journal of European Economic History*, VI (1977), pp. 663–4.

43 S. Fenoaltea, 'Italy', in P.K. O'Brien (ed.), *Railways and the*

Economic Development of Western Europe, London: Macmillan, 1983, pp. 49 *et seq.*

44 There is much evidence of a strong cyclical expansion in investments in public works in the new series constructed in S. Fenoaltea, 'Le opere pubbliche in Italia', in *Rivista della Storia Economica*, II (1985), pp. 335–69. See also S. Fenoaltea, 'Le costruzioni in Italia, 1861–1913', in *Rivista di Storia Economica*, IV (1987), pp. 1–34.

45 For a brief summary of these links see M. Fratianni and F. Spinelli, 'Currency Competition, Fiscal Policy and the Money Supply Process in Italy from Unification to World War I', in *The Journal of European Economic History*, XIV (1985), pp. 473–95.

46 G. Fuà (ed.), *Lo sviluppo economico in Italia*, Milan: Angeli, 1969, vol. III, pp. 389–90 and 432–3.

47 G. Brosio and C. Marchese, *Il potere di spendere. Economia e storia della spesa pubblica dall'Unificazione a oggi*, Bologna: Il Mulino, 1986, p. 54. The authors note that these were relatively high levels with respect to those of other countries, especially if Italy's lower level of income is taken into consideration.

48 A. Pedone, 'Il bilancio dello stato', in G. Fuà (ed.), op. cit., vol. II, p. 218.

49 It is debatable whether this policy contributed to the creation of private savings, the growth of which more probably depended on the increase in income.

50 'The Progress of Italian Finance', in *The Economist*, 31 January 1903, p. 38.

51 'Italian Budget', in *The Economist*, 14 December 1907, p. 2174.

52 See P. Ciocca, 'Note sulla politica monetaria italiana, 1900–1913', in G. Toniolo (ed.), *L'economia italiana 1861–1940*, Bari: Laterza, 1978, pp. 179–221.

53 ibid., p. 214.

54 These were Consols (Rendita Italiana) at 5 per cent gross and 4 per cent net.

55 P. Ciocca, op. cit., p. 216.

56 ibid., p. 217.

57 V. Zamagni, *Industrializzazione e squilibri regionali in Italia*, Bologna: Il Mulino, 1978.

58 Cf. J.G. Williamson, 'Regional Inequality and the Process of National Development: A Description of the Patterns', in *Economic Development and Cultural Change*, XIII (July 1965), pp. 3–84.

Chapter eleven: The War economy

1 L. Einaudi, *La condotta economica e gli effetti sociali della guerra italiana*, Bari: Laterza, 1933.

2 G. Fuà (ed.), *Lo sviluppo economico in Italia*, Milan: Franco Angeli, 1969, vol. III, p. 443.

3 Kindleberger recalls that, according to Keynes, 'in war the British

government gives its citizens tax receipts, the French give theirs *rentes*, and the Germans hand out money.' (C.P. Kindleberger, 'The Financial Aftermath of War', *Rivista di Storia Economica*, I (1984), International Issue, p. 120).

4 L. Einaudi, op. cit., p. 31.

5 Cf. G. Fuà (ed.), op. cit., p. 411. We have not included in the average of pre-War production that for 1913, which was exceptionally high.

6 L. Einaudi, op. cit., p. 83. Obviously this reduction in the labour force did not take place all at once: the peak was reached at the end of 1917. Exemptions for agricultural workers and leave granted to soldiers during harvest time slightly mitigated the reduction in the agricultural labour force.

7 L. Einaudi, *Cronache economiche e politiche di un trentennio*, Turin: Einaudi, 1961, vol. I, p. 206.

8 R. Romeo, *Breve storia della grande industria in Italia*, Bologna: Cappelli, 1972, p. 118.

9 Camera dei Deputati, 'Relazione della commissione parlamentare d'inchiesta per le spese di guerra', *Atti Parlamentari*, Legislature XXVI, Session 1921–3, Rome, 1923, p. 107.

10 R. Romeo, op. cit., p. 118.

11 Apart from the above-mentioned 'Commissione parlamentare d'inchiesta' (pp. 247–310), see also A. Caracciolo, 'Crescita e trasformazione della grande industria durante la prima guerra mondiale', in G. Fuà (ed.), op. cit., vol. II, pp. 237–8.

12 L. Einaudi, *La condotta economica e gli effetti sociali della guerra italiana*, Bari, Laterza, pp. 75–6.

13 A. Caracciolo, op. cit., p. 230.

14 ibid., p. 216. Ministerial Circular dated 27 June 1915 from General Dallolio.

15 A. De Stefani, *La legislazione economica della guerra*, Bari: Laterza, 1926, pp. 416–17.

16 Created on 8 June 1915.

17 A. Caracciolo, op. cit., p. 206.

18 L. Einaudi, *La condotta economica*, p. 105.

19 A. Caracciolo, op. cit., pp. 208–9.

20 The Commission, set up in 1920 and composed of fifteen senators and fifteen members of the Lower Chamber, published its report on 6 February 1923.

21 A. Caracciolo (op. cit., pp. 216–17) rightly notes that one of the elements in favour of the large firms was 'the widespread practice of putting persons closely connected with private enterprises in charge of government offices'. Among these were Crespi, Ferraris, Conti, and Pirelli.

22 If one looks at the increase in expenditure over that in 1913, an increase that can be attributed almost entirely to the War, the percentage of expenditure financed by taxation falls to 19 per cent. Data from G. Fuà (ed.), op. cit., pp. 442–3.

23 P. Sraffa, *L'inflazione monetaria in Italia durante e dopo la guerra*,

Milan: R. Università di Torino, 1920, p. 16.

24 Banks of issue were allowed to rediscount only bills endorsed by at least two people known to be solvent.

25 A.M. Biscaini, P. Gnes, A. Roselli, 'Origini e sviluppo del Consorzio per Sovvenzioni su Valori Industriali durante il Governatore Stringher', in *Bancaria*, February 1985.

26 That being endorsed by the Consortium itself became eligible for rediscount.

27 A.M. Biscaini, P. Gnes, A. Roselli, op. cit., Table 1.

28 Banca d'Italia, *Adunanza generale ordinaria degli azionisti*, Rome, 1920, p. 12.

29 On the various aspects of the domestic and foreign war finance and on the role of the Bank of Italy see G. Toniolo (ed.), *La Banca d'Italia e l'economia di guerra, 1914–19*, Rome: Laterta, 1990.

Chapter twelve: The economic development of Liberal Italy

1 A. Gramsci, *Il Risorgimento*, Turin: Einaudi, 1950, especially pp. 69–104.

2 E. Sereni, *Il capitalismo nelle campagne 1860–1900*, Turin: Einaudi, 1947.

3 See G. Orlando, *Storia della politica agraria in Italia dal 1848 a oggi*, Bari: Laterza, 1984.

4 E. Sereni, op. cit., p. 40.

5 ibid.

6 R. Romeo, *Risorgimento e capitalismo*, Bari, Laterza: 1959, p. 46.

7 ibid.

8 ibid.

9 ISTAT, 'Indagine statistica sullo sviluppo del reddito nazionale dell'Italia dal 1861 al 1957', in *Annali di Statistica*, series VIII, vol. 9, Rome, 1957.

10 A. Gerschenkron, *Economic Backwardness in Historical Perspective*, Cambridge, Mass.: Belknap Press, 1962, p. 7.

11 ibid., p. 8.

12 ibid., p. 73.

13 A. Confalonieri, *Banca e industria in Italia 1894–1906*, vol. I, Milan: Banca Commerciale Italiana, 1974.

14 S. Fenoaltea, 'Public Policy and Italian Industrial Development 1861–1913', unpublished doctoral thesis, Harvard University, 1967.

15 S. Fenoaltea, 'Riflessioni sull'esperienza industriale italiana dal Risorgimento alla prima guerra mondiale', in G. Toniolo (ed.), *L'economia italiana 1861–1940*, Bari: Laterza, 1978, pp. 93–103.

16 ibid., p. 78.

17 See also S. Fenoaltea, 'Decollo, ciclo, e intervento dello Stato', in A. Caracciolo (ed.), *La formazione dell'Italia industriale*, Bari: Laterza, 1969.

18 S. Fenoaltea, 'Riflessioni', p. 78.

19 ibid., p. 80.
20 ibid.
21 ibid.
22 ibid., p. 82.
23 ibid.
24 ibid., p. 83.
25 S. Fenoaltea, 'International Resource Flows and Construction Movements in the Atlantic Economy: the Kuznets Cycle in Italy, 1861–1913', *The Journal of Economic History*, XLVIII (1988), pp. 605–37.
26 S. Fenoaltea, 'Public Works Construction in Italy, 1861–1913', *Rivista di Storia Economica*, III (1986), International Issue, pp. 1–33; and S. Fenoaltea, 'Construction in Italy 1861–1913', *Rivista di Storia Economica*, IV (1987), International Issue, pp. 21–53.
27 S. Fenoaltea, 'International Resource Flows', p. 634.
28 ibid., pp. 634–5.
29 See G. Mori, 'Il tempo della protoindustrializzazione', in G. Mori (ed.), *L'industrializzazione in Italia (1861–1900)*, Bologna: Il Mulino, 1977.
30 L. Cafagna, 'The Industrial Revolution in Italy', in C.M. Cipolla (ed.), *The Fontana Economic History of Europe*, Glasgow, Fontana-Collins, 1973, vol. IV; and L. Cafagna, *Dualismo e sviluppo nella storia d'Italia*, Venice: Marsilio, 1989.
31 F. Bonelli, 'Il capitalismo italiano. Linee generali di interpretazione', in *Annali della Storia d'Italia Einaudi*, vol. I, Turin: Einaudi, 1978, pp. 1195–255. A good critical analysis of this work may be found in G. Federico, 'Di un nuovo modello dell'industrializzazione italiana', in *Società e Storia*, no. 8 (1980), pp. 443–55.
32 G. Mori, *Il capitalismo industriale in Italia*, Rome: Editori Riuniti, 1977, p. 21.
33 The most notable free-traders were Salvemini, Einaudi, De Viti-De Marco, Giretti, Fortunato, and Dorso. In the period around the First World War they gathered around Salvemini's weekly magazine *L'Unità*. The banner was later taken up by Einaudi's *Riforma Sociale*.
34 A. Gerschenkron, op. cit., p. 80.
35 ibid., p. 81.
36 S. Fenoaltea, 'Riflessioni', pp. 84–5.
37 G. Toniolo, 'Effective Protection and Industrial Growth: the Case of Italian Engineering, 1898–1913', in *The Journal of European Economic History*, VI (1977), pp. 659–73.
38 See F. Carli, *Produzioni naturali e produzioni nazionali*, Rome, 1914.
39 S. Lanaro, *Nazione e lavoro*, Venice: Marsilio, 1979, p. 182.
40 For an excellent summary of the terms of the debate see B. Caizzi (ed.), *Nuova antologia della questione meridionale*, Milan: Comunità, 1962.
41 See E.M. Capecelatro and A. Carlo, *Contro la 'questione meridionale'*, Rome: Samonà e Savelli, 1972.
42 F.S. Nitti, 'Scritti sulla questione meridionale', in *Opere*, vol. II, Bari: Laterza, 1958.

43 G. Fortunato, *Il Mezzogiorno e lo Stato Italiano*, Florence: Vallecchi, no date, vol. II, p. 318, quoted in B. Caizzi, op. cit., p. 32.
44 P. Saraceno, *L'Italia verso la piena occupazione*, Milan: Feltrinelli, 1963, p. 15.
45 The best critical summary of this interpretation may be found in R. Villari, *Mezzogiorno e democrazia*, Bari: Laterza, 1979.
46 L. Cafagna, 'Intorno alle origini del dualismo economico', in (various authors) *Saggi in onore di Leopoldo Cassese*, Naples, 1971.
47 See S. Fenoaltea, 'Ferrovie e sviluppo industriale italiano 1861–1913', in G. Toniolo (ed.), *L'economia italiana 1861–1940*, Bari: Laterza, 1978, pp. 105–54.
48 P. Saraceno, op. cit., p. 21.
49 V. Zamagni, *Industrializzazione e squilibri regionali in Italia*, Bologna: Il Mulino, 1978.
50 A. Maddison, *Phases of Capitalist Development*, Oxford: Oxford University Press, 1982, pp. 86 *et seq.*
51 Apart from the work of Romeo already mentioned, see also G. Are, *Alle origini dell'Italia industriale*, Naples: Guida, 1974; and G. Are, *Lo sviluppo industriale nell'età della destra*, Pisa: Nistri-Lischi, 1965.
52 See Chapter four.
53 R. Vivarelli, *Il fallimento del liberalismo*, Bologna: Il Mulino, 1981, pp. 338–9.
54 S. Lanaro, op. cit., pp. 8–9.
55 ibid.
56 See G. Toniolo, *L'economia dell'Italia fascista*, Bari: Laterza, 1980.

Index

Notes. Some references to names of people are to quotations from their work, although their names may not be given on the pages. Sub-entries are in alphabetical order, except where chronological order is significant.

Index

Balduino, Domenico 58
Banca Commerciale Italiana
  (Comit) 24, 113–15, 132, 139
Banca di Credito Italiano 59
Banca Generale 64, 76, 89, 90–2,
  95, 96, 113, 140
Banca di Genova 113
Banca d'Italia 23, 94–7, 114–16,
  119–20, 132
Banca Italiana di Sconto 24, 117,
  127, 132
Banca di Milano 91
Banca Nazionale nel Regno (Later
  in Banca d'Italia) 62, 63–4, 80,
  91, 92–4
Banca Nazionale degli Stati Sardi
  (later Banca Nazionale nel
  Regno) 47, 57–8
Banca Nazionale Toscana (later in
  Banca d'Italia) 57, 92–4
Banca Romana 57, 89, 91–5, 97
  114, 119
Banca Sarda 58
Banca di Sconto e Sete 59, 89, 90,
  91
Banca di Sicilia 94
Banca Tiberina 89, 90, 91
Banca di Torino 76–7
Banca Toscana du Credito (later
  in Banca d'Italia) 57, 92–4
Banche Popolari 77
Banco di Napoli 91, 94
Banco di Roma 24, 132
Banking Acts (1874, 1893) 92, 94,
  95, 119
banks: before Unification 22–4,
  47; in Right, age of 62, 64; and
  contradictions of 1880s 76–7,
  80–1; in crisis decade 88–9,
  90–7; failures and scandals 23,
  86, 90–2; in Giolitti age
  113–17, 119–20; in First World
  War 23, 127, 130, 132;
  interpretaions of economic
  development 139–40, 147; and
  monetary unification 57–9
Banque d'Escompte 80
Barbieri, I.B. 33

Baring 89, 90
Bastogi (Finance Minister) 55–6,
  61
Bava-Beccaris, General 106
Belgium: GDP 99; industry 68, 69;
  per capita income 50, 157;
  railways 50; trade with 46
Biagini (of Treasury) 91, 95
Biella 109
birth rates 26–7, 36
Biscaini Cotula, A.M. 23–4
Bologna 65
Bonaparte, Joseph 38–9
Bonelli, F. 94, 142–3
Bourbons 41, 56
bourgeoisie, lack of effective
  135–6, 150
Brazil 112
Breda 75, 107, 127
budget: balancing 18; deficit *see*
  debt; policy *see* economic
  policy, fiscal policy *and*
  monetary policy

Cafagna, L. 41, 142–3, 148
Cairoli, B. 82
Cambray-Digny (Finance Minister)
  61
Canada 99
Candeloro, G. 51, 86
capital 25; accumulation 17;
  foreign 81, 87, 88–9, 102;
  formation 2; for industry 76–8;
  lack of 137, 138; product per
  unit of 29–31; social overhead
  see public works; stock 15; *see
  also* investment
Caporetto defeat 131–2
Caracciolo, A. 42, 44
Carcano, P. (Treasury) 116
Carli, F. 146
Carlo Alberto, King 1, 39
Carlo Felice, King 39
Carocci, G. 48–9, 70
Cassa Depositi e Prestiti 47
Castronovo, V. 70
Catholic movement 70–1, 106
Cavour, Count C.B. di 39, 48, 70